IN THE NAME O

ALLAH

THE ALL-COMPASSIONATE, ALL-MERCIFUL

FUNERAL RITES IN ISLAM

- Title: FUNERAL RITES IN ISLAM
- Author: Dr. Abu Ameenah Bilal Philips
- English Edition 2: 2005
- Layout: IIPH, Riyadh, Saudi Arabia
- Filming & Cover Designing: Samo Press Group

Revised Edition

FUNERAL RITES IN ISLAM

Dr. Abu Ameenah Bilal Philips

INTERNATIONAL ISLAMIC PUBLISHING HOUSE

King Fahd National Library Cataloging-in-Publication Data

Philips, Abu Ameenah Bilal
Funeral rites in Islam. / Abu Ameenah Bilal Philips ; 2nd ed., - Riyadh , 2005

...p ; 22 cm

ISBN: **9960-850-84-6**

1- Funeral rites and ceremonies. Islamic I-Title

252.9 dc 1424/6812

Legal deposit no. **1424/6812**
ISBN: **9960-850-84-6**

International Islamic Publishing House (IIPH)
P.O.Box 55195 Riyadh 11534, Saudi Arabia
Tel: 966 1 4650818 - 4647213 - Fax: 4633489
E-Mail: iiphiiph.com.sa . www.iiph.com.sa

TABLE OF CONTENTS

PUBLISHER'S NOTE

All praise and thanks belong to Allah alone, the One, the All-High, All-Merciful. Blessings and Peace be upon Prophet Muhammad, the last of His messengers and prophets, his family, his Companions and all those who follow in his footsteps till the end of time.

Death is the ultimate reality of life. This life is only a transitory phase on the way to Paradise or Hell as the case may be. Islam being the complete code of life has a set of complete instructions both for the dying individuals and the people around him/her who will be performing the burial rites.

Due to the great impact of non-Islamic inroads into the Muslim society, people in general have drifted away from the Sunnah way of treating the dying and the deceased. Dr. Abu Ameenah Bilal Philips has compiled this book to cater to the needs of the English speaking Muslims in a brief and easy to understand language based strictly on the basic sources of Islam, the Qur'an and Sunnah.

This is a thoroughly revised edition of the book by the author and we are happy to present it to our English readers in the best possible form. May Allah bless the efforts of all who contributed to the production of the book with acceptance.

Muhammad ibn 'Abdul-Muhsin al-Tuwaijri

General Manager,
International Islamic Publishing House, IIPH
Riyadh, Saudi Arabia

FOREWORD

Although death is not a pleasant or popular topic of discussion, it is absolutely the most certain event which every human being knows must happen in his or her life. Consequently, Islam has provided a complete set of instructions for the dying individual, those who are present at the time of death, as well as those responsible for burying the deceased. These instructions should be common knowledge among Muslims, since death often comes when it is least expected. The purpose of this book is to provide English-speaking Muslims with a concise and authentic compilation of the instruction regarding funeral rites in Islam.

Books of this type are of particular importance today, because most Muslim communities, worldwide, have drifted far away from the pure teachings of Islam. As a result, much of their funeral rites consist of innovative practices absorbed from neighbouring non-Muslim communities or inherited from earlier generations of ignorant Muslims.

The material for this book was originally prepared in 1982-1983 for Book Three (Grade 9) of my Islamic Studies series which I taught for almost ten years at *Manaret al-Riyadh Arabic-Islamic* School. The main source of the information for the chapter was the classic, *Aḥkām al-Janā'iz* by Shaykh Nāṣirud-Dīn al-Albānī. The significance of Shaykh Nāṣir's work is, that it is both comprehensive, as well as fully authenticated. What is presently in the reader's hands is a summary of the main summary of the main issues related to Islamic funeral rites and the evidences used to prove them.

It was my intention to publish the chapter as a book on funeral rites a number of years ago. However, there were already some books available on the subject in English, so I chose to concentrate my publishing efforts in other fields where there was a greater lack of literature. The fact that I have now decided to publish this book does not mean that all the other areas in which there is a scarcity of authentic literature have now been completely covered. It is just that the need for such a text has been impressed on me repeatedly over the past few years. This is mainly due to the increased awareness of Muslims, over the past decade, about the importance of authentic writings.

Perhaps the best and most comprehensive book on the topic of funeral rites is volume four of the English translation of Sayyid Sabiq's *Fiqh as-Sunnah*.[1] However, there remains a need for a more rigorous authentication of the material used in the text. Also, volume four is part of an expensive five volume set, only available in hardback. Consequently, this work fills two voids; that of a fully authenticated work of funeral etiquette, and one that is reasonably priced.

In closing, I would like to thank all those who contributed to the publication of this book. Foremost among them are my proofreaders, like Sister Jamīlah Campbell and my wife, and my researchers, 'Abdul Majīd Ḥasan, who helped greatly in providing the hadith references in English sources, and Riaz Ansary, who helped edit the final text. Finally, I ask Allah to record this work among my good deeds and reward all who contributed to its publication.

Dr. Abu Amīnah Bilal Philips
Sharjah, U.A.E.

---

[1] Originally published by American Trust Publications, Indianapolis, USA.

CHAPTER 1: THE TIME OF DYING

When one finds oneself on his or her deathbed, or what appears to be the deathbed, one is obliged or recommended to do certain acts of worship, and the people around the dying individual are encouraged to be supportive and to provide certain basic services.

1) The *Shahādah*

Those present should encourage the dying person to repeat after them the Declaration of Faith (*Shahādah*), confirming Allah's unique oneness (*tawḥīd*), until he or she passes away. Both Abu Sa'īd al-Khudri and Abu Hurayrah quoted the Prophet (Blessings and Peace be upon him) as saying,

((لَقِّنُوا مَوْتَاكُمْ لاَ إِلَهَ إِلاَّ اللَّهُ وَمَنْ كَانَ آخِرُ كَلاَمِهِ لاَ إِلَهَ إِلاَّ اللَّهُ عِنْدَ الْمَوْتِ دَخَلَ الْجَنَّةَ يَوْمًا مِنَ الدَّهْرِ ، وَإِنْ أَصَابَهُ قَبْلَ ذَلِكَ مَا أَصَابَهُ .))

> *"Prompt your dying ones (to say): lā ilāha il-lal-lāh;*[2] *and whoever's last words before dying are: lā ilāha il-lal-lāh, will enter Paradise one day, even if he is afflicted before that by punishment."*[3]

---

[2] Muslim (English trans), vol. 2, p. 435, hadith no. 1996, *Sunan Abi Dāwūd*, vol. 2, p. 887, hadith no. 3111, *Sunan Ibn Mājah*, vol. 2, p. 365, hadith no. 1444, *Mishkāt al-Maṣābīḥ*, vol. 1, p. 337 and *Riyadh-uṣ-Ṣaleḥīn*, vol. 2, p. 474, hadith no. 918.

[3] This addition is only found in *Ṣaḥīḥ ibn Ḥibbān* and it is authenticated by Shaykh al-Albāni in *Irwā al-Ghalīl*, vol. 3, p. 150.

This prophetic statement does not simply mean that the *Shahādah* should be mentioned by others in the presence of the one who is dying. The dying person, himself or herself should be instructed to say the *Shahādah*, as is evident from the Prophet's statement, "*Before dying are: lā ilāha il-lal-lāh will enter Paradise one day...*" The following hadith, narrated by Anas, indicates the Prophet's practice in this regard:

عَنْ أَنَسِ بْنِ مَالِكٍ أَنَّ رَسُولَ اللَّهِ ﷺ عَادَ رَجُلاً مِنَ الْأَنْصَارِ فَقَالَ: ((يَا خَالُ قُلْ لاَ إِلَهَ إِلاَّ اللَّهُ)). فَقَالَ: أَخَالٌ أَمْ عَمٌّ؟ فَقَالَ: ((لاَ بَلْ خَالٌ)). قَالَ: فَخَيْرٌ لِي أَنْ أَقُولَ لاَ إِلَهَ إِلاَّ اللَّهُ؟ فَقَالَ النَّبِيُّ ﷺ: ((نَعَمْ)).

Anas ibn Mālik reported that the Messenger of Allah (ﷺ) visited a man from among the Anṣār and said to him, "*O Uncle, say: lā ilāha il-lal-lāh.*" The man asked, "Am I a maternal uncle or a paternal uncle?" The Prophet (ﷺ) replied, "*Indeed you are maternal.*" The man then asked, "Is it better for me to say: *lā ilāha il-lal-lāh*?" The Prophet replied, "*Yes.*"[4]

Muslims are also encouraged to be present when non-Muslims are dying in order to present Islam to them, in the hope that they will accept Islam prior to their deaths. For the acceptance of Islam at this point to be of any benefit, it must be based on knowledge,[5] it must be expressed sincerely[6] and with

[4] Collected by Aḥmad and authenticated in *al-Fatḥ ar-Rabbāni*, vol. 7, p. 57, hadith no. 34, as well as in *Aḥkām al-Janā'iz*, p. 11.

((فَاعْلَمُواْ أَنَّهُ لاَ إِلَهَ إِلاَّ اللُّه))

[5] ﴾Know that there is no god worthy of worship besides Allah.﴿ *(Qur'an 47: 19).*

((وَمَا أُمِرُواْ إِلاَّ لِيَعْبُدُواْ اللَّه مُخْلِصِينَ لَهُ الدِّينَ))

[6] ﴾They were only commanded to worship Allah, making the religion sincere for Him alone.﴿ (*Qur'an 98: 5).*

certainty,[7] and it must take place before the actual throes of death begin.[8] This point is evident in the Prophet's attempt to get his uncle Abu Ṭālib to bear witness to Allah's oneness when the latter was on his deathbed.[9] Abu Ṭālib knew about Allah, Islam, and the Prophet (ﷺ) very well. Similarly, the following incident involving the Prophet's servant is one of a person who knew about Allah and the Prophet.

عَنْ أَنَسٍ رضي الله عنه قَالَ: كَانَ غُلَامٌ يَهُودِيٌّ يَخْدُمُ النَّبِيَّ ﷺ فَمَرِضَ فَأَتَاهُ النَّبِيُّ ﷺ يَعُودُهُ فَقَعَدَ عِنْدَ رَأْسِهِ فَقَالَ لَهُ: ((أَسْلِمْ)). فَنَظَرَ إِلَى أَبِيهِ وَهُوَ عِنْدَهُ فَقَالَ لَهُ أَطِعْ أَبَا الْقَاسِمِ ﷺ ، فَأَسْلَمَ فَخَرَجَ النَّبِيُّ ﷺ وَهُوَ يَقُولُ: ((الْحَمْدُ لِلَّهِ الَّذِي أَنْقَذَهُ مِنَ النَّارِ)). [فلما مات ، قال: ((صلوا على صاحبكم)).

Anas also narrated, "When a Jewish youth who used to serve the Prophet got sick, the Prophet (ﷺ) visited him. The Prophet (ﷺ) sat by his head and said to him, "*Accept Islam.*" The boy looked at his father who was near him, and the man said, "Obey Abul-Qāsim." So the boy accepted Islam and the Prophet (ﷺ) left saying, "*All praise is due to Allah, who saved him from the Fire.*"[10] [When the boy died, the Prophet (Blessings and Peace be

---

[7] Abu Hurayrah reported Allah's Messenger (ﷺ) as saying, "*I testify that there is no god worthy of worship but Allah and that I am the Messenger of Allah. Any servant who meets Allah with those two (testimonies), having no doubt in them*, will enter Paradise." [Muslim (English trans), vol. 1, p. 20, hadith no. 41].

[8] The Prophet (ﷺ) is reported by ʻAbdullah ibn ʻUmar to have said, "*Allah, Most Great and Glorious, will accept His servant's repentance until the throes of death begin.*" (Collected by Tirmidhi and Ibn Mājah and authenticated by Shaykh al-Albāni in *Ṣaḥīḥ Sunan Ibn Mājah*, vol. 2, p. 418, hadith no. 3430. See *Riyadh-uṣ-Ṣaleḥīn*, vol. 1, p. 12, hadith no. 18, for an English translation of this hadith).

[9] Muslim (English trans), vol. 1, p. 18, hadith no. 36.

[10] Bukhari (Arabic-English), vol. 2, p. 246, hadith no. 438, *Sunan Abi Dāwūd*, vol. 2, Pp. 881-82, hadith no. 3089 and *Mishkāt al-Maṣābīḥ*, vol. 1, p. 328.

upon him) said, "*Make ṣalāh for your comrade.*"][11]

2) Good Words

People present may pray aloud for the one who is dying, letting the person hear their words of concern and sympathy. Those present should also avoid saying anything in the dying person's presence which is inappropriate. Negative words will only increase the difficulties which the sick and dying are facing. On the other hand, good words and positive thoughts will make the process of dying easier and the recovery from illness more bearable.

عَنْ أُمِّ سَلَمَةَ قَالَتْ: قَالَ رَسُولُ اللَّهِ ﷺ : ((إِذَا حَضَرْتُمُ الْمَرِيضَ أَوِ الْمَيِّتَ فَقُولُوا خَيْرًا فَإِنَّ الْمَلاَئِكَةَ يُؤَمِّنُونَ عَلَى مَا تَقُولُونَ)).

Umm Salamah related that the Prophet (ﷺ) said,

> *"If you are in the presence of a sick or dying person, you should say good things, for verily the angels say "Āmīn" to whatever you say."*[12]

When Umm Salamah asked the Prophet (ﷺ) what should she say, he replied,

((قُولِي اللَّهُمَّ اغْفِرْ لِي وَلَهُ وَأَعْقِبْنِي مِنْهُ عُقْبَى حَسَنَةً)).

> *"Say: Allahumma-ghfir li wa lahu wa a'qibni minhu 'uqbā ḥasanah (O Allah, forgive him and me, and grant*

---

[11] This addition is found in *Musnad Aḥmad* and is authenticated in *Aḥkām al-Janā'iz*, p. 11.

[12] Muslim (English trans) vol. 2, p. 436, hadith no. 2002. *Sunan Abi Dāwūd*, vol. 2, p. 887. hadith no. 3109, *Sunan Ibn Mājah*, vol. 2, Pp. 366-7, hadith no. 1447 and *Mishkāt al-Maṣābīḥ*, vol. 1, p. 337.

me a good substitute after him.)"[13]

3) *Sūrah Yāsīn*

The practice of specifically reading the 36th chapter of the Qur'an, *Sūrah Yāsīn*, in the presence of the dying has no basis in the authentic Sunnah.[14] Neither the Prophet (ﷺ) nor his Companions did it, or recommended that it be done. However, it does fall under the general heading of 'good things' which could be said in the presence of one who is dying, but it carries with it no special value. Reciting this chapter is like reciting any other chapter in the Qur'an. Consequently, one may read it for the dying, if one wishes to do so, or if the dying person requests it due to his or her personal preference for it. However, to specify that *Sūrah Yāsīn* should be read for the dying and to believe that doing so has special value is considered *bid'ah*, a sinful innovation in the religion.

4) Facing Qiblah

Turning the body of one who is dying so that he or she faces the *qiblah* (Makkah) has no foundation in the practice of the Prophet (ﷺ) and his Companions. The body should be turned to face Makkah when it is placed in the grave, according to the Prophet's instructions. However, at the time of dying, there were no such instructions. Turning the body became a custom after the time of the Prophet's Companions, but was objected to by the scholars of

---

[13] Muslim (English trans), vol. 2, p. 436, hadith no. 2002.

[14] There is an inauthentic hadith to that effect narrated by Ma'qil and collected in *Sunan Abi Dāwūd*, vol. 2, p. 889, hadith no. 3115. *Sunan Ibn Mājah*, vol. 2, p. 367 hadith no. 1448. See also *Mishkāt al-Maṣābīḥ*, vol. 1, p. 338. It is declared inauthentic in *Ḍa'īf Sunan Abi Dāwūd*, p. 316, hadith no. 683.

that time. For example, Sa'īd ibn al-Musayyib,[15] one of the leading scholars among the students of the Prophet's Companions, openly expressed his dislike for this practice. Zar'ah ibn 'Abdir-Raḥmān reported that he saw Abu Salamah ibn 'Abdir-Raḥmān with Sa'īd ibn al-Musayyib when he was on his deathbed. When Sa'īd lost consciousness, Abu Salamah instructed that his bed be turned towards the Ka'bah. When Sa'īd regained consciousness he asked, "Did you move my bed?" When they replied that they had done so, he looked at Abu Salamah and asked, "I think it was done with your knowledge?" He replied, "I told them to do so." Then Sa'īd instructed them to return his bed to its original position.[16]

5) Acceptance of Fate

The dying individual is obliged to accept his lot gracefully so that it becomes a source of reward and blessing for him on the Day of Judgment. The Prophet (ﷺ) taught that patiently bearing the trials of this life is an act of righteousness which expiates sins.

عَنْ عَبْدِاللَّهِ قَالَ: دَخَلْتُ عَلَى رَسُولِ اللَّهِ ﷺ وَهُوَ يُوعَكُ فَقُلْتُ: يَا رَسُولَ اللَّهِ إِنَّكَ لَتُوعَكُ وَعْكًا شَدِيدًا . قَالَ: ((أَجَلْ ، إِنِّي أُوعَكُ كَمَا يُوعَكُ رَجُلَانِ مِنْكُمْ)). قُلْتُ: ذَلِكَ أَنَّ لَكَ أَجْرَيْنِ قَالَ: ((أَجَلْ

---

[15] Sa'īd ibn al-Musayyib ibn Ḥazn (634-713CE), from the Madīnite tribe of Makhzūm, was one of the seven leading legal scholars of Madīnah. He was known as the most knowledgeable scholar —Ā'lam —about 'Umar ibn al-Khaṭṭāb's legal principles and his rulings. He lived on what he earned from the sale of olive oil and never accepted grants. (*Al-A'lām*, vol. 3, p. 155.)

[16] Collected by Ibn Abi Shaybah in *al-Muṣannaf* and authenticated in *Aḥkām al-Janā'iz*, p. 11, nt. 15.

ذَلِكَ . كَذَلِكَ مَا مِنْ مُسْلِمٍ يُصِيبُهُ أَذًى شَوْكَةٌ فَمَا فَوْقَهَا إِلاَّ كَفَّرَ اللَّهُ بِهَا سَيِّئَاتِهِ كَمَا تَحُطُّ الشَّجَرَةُ وَرَقَهَا)).

'Abdullah stated that he visited Allah's Messenger (ﷺ) while he was suffering from a high fever and said to him, "O Messenger of Allah, you have a high fever." He replied, "*Yes, I have a fever equal to what two of your men experience.*" I asked, "Is it because you will have double the reward?" He replied,

> "*Yes, it is so. Any Muslim who is afflicted with the harm of a thorn prick or more will have, as a result of it, some of his sins expiated the way a tree sheds its leaves.*"[17]

Expressing pity for those dying is counterproductive, because pity only makes it more difficult for those dying to accept their fate. Instead, those on their deathbed should be encouraged to think positively by being told that they are fortunate. They should be informed that, according to the Prophet (ﷺ), Allah has chosen them for a special reward.

عن أَبِي هُرَيْرَةَ يَقُولُ: قَالَ رَسُولُ اللَّهِ ﷺ : ((مَنْ يُرِدِ اللَّهُ بِهِ خَيْرًا يُصِبْ مِنْهُ)).

Abu Hurayrah stated that Allah's Messenger (ﷺ) said, "*Allah aflicts whomsoever He wishes good, with trials.*"[18]

Those on their deathbeds should be instructed to avoid questions like, "Why me?" and statements like, "I'm too young to die!" and "It's not fair!" as all of these indicate *kufr* (disbelief). They should be reminded that it is all for the best, if only they remain patient.

---

[17] Bukhari (Arabic-English), vol. 7, p. 374, hadith no. 551, and Muslim (English trans), vol. 4, p. 1364, hadith no. 6235.

[18] Bukhari (Arabic-English), vol. 7, p. 373, hadith no. 548.

عَنْ صُهَيْبٍ قَالَ: قَالَ رَسُولُ اللَّهِ ﷺ :((عَجَبًا لِأَمْرِ الْمُؤْمِنِ إِنَّ أَمْرَهُ كُلَّهُ خَيْرٌ وَلَيْسَ ذَاكَ لِأَحَدٍ إِلاَّ لِلْمُؤْمِنِ إِنْ أَصَابَتْهُ سَرَّاءُ شَكَرَ فَكَانَ خَيْرًا لَهُ وَإِنْ أَصَابَتْهُ ضَرَّاءُ صَبَرَ فَكَانَ خَيْرًا لَهُ)).

Ṣuhayb quoted the Prophet (ﷺ) as saying,

> *"The believer's affair is amazing; it is all for the good, and that is not the case of anyone besides the believer. If good times come to him, he is thankful and thus it is good for him, and if bad times befall him, he is patient and, thus, it is also good for him."*[19]

The dying individuals should also have good thoughts about Allah and be convinced that Allah has chosen the most appropriate time and way for them to die. In that way, they are able to protect their faith from doubts and fears.

عَنْ جَابِرِ بْنِ عَبْدِ اللَّهِ الأَنْصَارِيِّ قَالَ: سَمِعْتُ رَسُولَ اللَّهِ ﷺ قَبْلَ مَوْتِهِ بِثَلاثَةِ أَيَّامٍ يَقُولُ: ((لاَ يَمُوتَنَّ أَحَدُكُم إِلاَّ وَهُوَ يُحْسِنُ الظَّنَّ بِاللَّهِ عَزَّ وَجَلَّ)).

Jābir ibn 'Abdillah reported that three days before Allah's Messenger's death, he heard him say,

> *"All of you should die thinking about Allah in the best way."*[20]

Among those who may die with bad thoughts about Allah are those who were only cultural Muslims. They only perform some

---

[19] Muslim (English trans), vol. 4, p. 1541, hadith no. 7138. See also *Mishkāt al-Maṣābīḥ*, vol. 2, p. 1098.

[20] Muslim (English trans), vol. 4, p. 1492, hadith no. 6877, *Sunan Abi Dāwūd*, vol. 2, p. 886, hadith no. 3107, and *Mishkāt al-Maṣābīḥ*, vol. 1, p. 334.

of the Islamic rites and rituals because it is the custom of their people. However, they never accepted true faith in their hearts throughout their lives. Consequently when death approaches, they will not want to accept their fate, and their deathbed doubts will often tear down their false claims of belief, leaving them expressing statements of clear disbelief as death overcomes them. It may be a big surprise for those present around them, for everyone assumed that they were Muslims destined for Paradise, based on their ritual observance of some or most of the basic religious rites. Prophet Muhammad (ﷺ) addressed this phenomenon as follows:

عَنْ سَهْلِ بْنِ سَعْدٍ السَّاعِدِيِّ أَنَّ رَسُولَ اللَّهِ ﷺ قَالَ: ((إِنَّ الرَّجُلَ لَيَعْمَلُ عَمَلَ أَهْلِ الْجَنَّةِ فِيمَا يَبْدُو لِلنَّاسِ وَهُوَ مِنْ أَهْلِ النَّارِ)).

Sahl ibn Sa'd reported that the Prophet (ﷺ) said,

> *"Indeed a man may appear to people to do the deeds of the people of Paradise, yet he will be among the people of Hell."*[21]

In another narration, Abu Hurayrah narrated that the Prophet (ﷺ) said,

> *"Surely, a person may do the deeds of the people of Paradise for a long time, then terminate his deeds with the deeds of the people of Hell."*[22]

Since everyone's deeds were already recorded in the book of destiny prior to the creation of the world, the Prophet (ﷺ) also referred to the change in deeds from good to bad as the record or destiny overtaking the individual.

---

[21] Muslim (English trans), vol. 4, p. 1395, hadith no. 6408.

[22] Ibid, p. 1394, hadith no. 6407.

عن عبد الله بن مسعود قال : قال رسول الله ﷺ وهو الصادق المصدوق : ((إِنَّ أَحَدَكُمْ لَيَعْمَلُ بِعَمَلِ أَهْلِ الْجَنَّةِ حَتَّى لاَ يَكُونُ بَيْنَهَا وَبَيْنَهُ إِلاَّ ذِرَاعٌ فَيَسْبِقُ عَلَيْهِ الْكِتَابُ فَيَعْمَلُ بِعَمَلِ أَهْلِ النَّارِ فَيَدْخُلُ النَّارَ))

'Abdullah ibn Mas'ūd related that Allah's Messenger (ﷺ), the truthful, said,

> *"One of you may do the deeds of the people of Paradise until only an arm's length remains between him and Paradise, then what was written overtakes him and he does the deeds of the people of Hell and enters Hell."*[23]

6) Between Fear and Hope

The dying person should be in a psychological state between fear and hope. The person should fear Allah's punishment for his or her sins and, at the same time, hope for Allah's mercy and forgiveness. The true believer is not sure about whether he or she is going to Paradise, no matter how good his or her life may have been, because the Prophet (ﷺ) said that no one would enter Paradise solely on the basis of good deeds.[24] Every human makes many errors during his or her lifetime. Although a person may consider some of his or her errors insignificant, they may have had exceedingly bad results. The dying person also should not give up hope in Allah's mercy, no matter how great his or her sins may have been, for Allah is able to forgive all sins, as He said,

---

[23] Bukhari (Arabic-English), vol. 9, Pp. 411-2, hadith no. 546, and Muslim (English trans), vol. 4, p. 1391, hadith no. 6390.

[24] Muslim (English trans), vol. 4, Pp. 1473-4, hadith nos. 6390 & 6770.

﴿... لَا تَقْنَطُوا۟ مِن رَّحْمَةِ ٱللَّهِ ۚ إِنَّ ٱللَّهَ يَغْفِرُ ٱلذُّنُوبَ جَمِيعًا ۚ ... ﴿٥٣﴾﴾ (سورة الزمر : ٥٣)

﴿...Do not lose hope of Allah's mercy, for verily Allah [can] forgive all sins...﴾ (Qur'an 39: 53)

The only exception to that rule is the sin of *shirk*, as it negates the very purpose of creation:

﴿إِنَّ ٱللَّهَ لَا يَغْفِرُ أَن يُشْرَكَ بِهِۦ وَيَغْفِرُ مَا دُونَ ذَٰلِكَ لِمَن يَشَآءُ ۚ... ﴿٤٨﴾﴾ (سورة النساء : ٤٨ ، ١١٦)

﴿Verily Allah will not forgive *shirk*, but He forgives anything besides it to whomsoever He wishes...﴾ (Qur'an 4: 48 and 116)

عَنْ أَنَسٍ أَنَّ النَّبِيَّ صَلَّى اللَّهم عَلَيْهِ وَسَلَّمَ دَخَلَ عَلَى شَابٍّ وَهُوَ فِي الْمَوْتِ فَقَالَ: ((كَيْفَ تَجِدُكَ))؟ قَالَ: واللَّهَ يَا رَسُولَ اللَّهِ إني أرجو الله واني وَأَخَافُ ذُنُوبِي. فَقَالَ رَسُولُ اللَّهِ ﷺ: ((لاَ يَجْتَمِعَانِ فِي قَلْبِ عَبْدٍ فِي مِثْلِ هَذَا الْمَوْطِنِ إِلاَّ أَعْطَاهُ اللَّهُ مَا يَرْجُو وَآمَنَهُ مِمَّا يَخَافُ)).

Anas stated that the Prophet (ﷺ) visited a dying youth and asked him, "How do you find yourself?" He replied, "By Allah, O Messenger of Allah, verily I hope for the best from Allah and fear the consequences of my sins." Allah's Messenger (ﷺ) said,

> *"Whenever these two (hope and fear) come together in the heart of a slave (of Allah), in such a situation, Allah gives him what he hopes for and protects him from what he fears."*[25]

---

25 Collected by Tirmidhi and Ibn Mājah and authenticated in *Aḥkām al-Janā'iz*, p. 3, nt. 2. See *Mishkāt al-Maṣābīḥ*, vol. 1, p. 335 for the English text.

7) The Death Wish

No matter how severe the pain of the sickness may become, one is not allowed to hope or wish for death. The death wish reflects a belief that Allah has burdened one beyond his capacity and indicates a lack of patience. The longer people live, the more opportunity they have to do good and improve their lot.

عَنْ أُمِّ الْفَضْلِ أَنَّ رَسُولَ اللَّه ﷺ دَخَلَ عَلَيهِمْ، وَعَبَّاس عَمُّ رَسُولِ اللَّهِ يَشْتَكِي، فَتَمَنَّى عَبَّاس الْمَوْتَ ، فَقَالَ لَهُ رَسُولُ اللَّهِ ﷺ : ((يَا عَمِّ! لاَ تَتَمَنَّ الْمَوتَ، فَإِنَّكَ إِنْ كُنْتَ مُحْسِنًا، فَأَنْ تُؤَخَّرَ تَزْدَادُ إِحْسَانًا إِلَى إِحْسَانِكَ خَيْر لَكَ، وَإِنْ كُنْتَ مُسِيْئًا فَأَنْ تُؤخَّرَ فَتَسْتَعْتِبُ مِنْ إِسَائَتِكَ خَيْر لَكَ، فَلاَ تَتَمَنَّ الْمَوْتَ)).

Umm al-Faḍl reported that the Prophet (ﷺ) came to see them while the Prophet's uncle 'Abbās was complaining (of his sickness). When 'Abbās wished for death, the Prophet (ﷺ) told him,

> *"O uncle, don't wish for death, for verily if you were good and your death is delayed, it will add more good to your previous goodness and it will be better for you; and if you were bad it will be better for you that your death be delayed so you may find fault in your bad deeds (and seek forgiveness). So don't wish for death."*[26]

عَنْ أَنَسِ بْنِ مَالِكٍ رضي الله عنه قَالَ النَّبِيُّ ﷺ : ((لاَ يَتَمَنَّيَنَّ أَحَدُكُمُ الْمَوْتَ مِنْ ضُرٍّ أَصَابَهُ فَإِنْ كَانَ لاَ بُدَّ فَاعِلاً فَلْيَقُلِ اللَّهُمَّ أَحْيِنِي مَا كَانَتِ الْحَيَاةُ خَيْرًا لِي وَتَوَفَّنِي إِذَا كَانَتِ الْوَفَاةُ خَيْرًا لِي)).

---

[26] This narration is found in *al-Mustadrak*, vol. 1, p. 339, and is authenticated in *Aḥkām al-Janā'iz*, p. 4.

Anas quoted the Prophet (ﷺ) as saying,

> *"None of you should wish for death because of some harm which has afflicted him. But if one must do it, let him say: Allahumma aḥyini mā kānatil-ḥayātu khayran li (O Allah keep me alive as long as living is best for me) wa tawaffani idhā kānatil-wafātu khayran li (and take my life if death is better for me)."*[27]

8) Debts

Dying individuals may have in their possession certain items belonging to others. If that is the case, they should return them if they are able to do so, in order to avoid having to repay them from their good deeds on the Day of Judgment. The Prophet (ﷺ) warned his followers of this reality as follows:

عَنْ أَبِي هُرَيْرَةَ رضي الله عنه قَالَ: قَالَ رَسُولُ اللَّهِ ﷺ: ((مَنْ كَانَتْ لَهُ مَظْلَمَةٌ لِأَخِيهِ مِنْ عِرْضِهِ أَوْ شَيْءٍ فَلْيَتَحَلَّلْهُ مِنْهُ الْيَوْمَ قَبْلَ أَنْ لاَ يَكُونَ دِينَارٌ وَلاَ دِرْهَمٌ إِنْ كَانَ لَهُ عَمَلٌ صَالِحٌ أُخِذَ مِنْهُ بِقَدْرِ مَظْلَمَتِهِ وَإِنْ لَمْ تَكُنْ لَهُ حَسَنَاتٌ أُخِذَ مِنْ سَيِّئَاتِ صَاحِبِهِ فَحُمِلَ عَلَيْهِ)).

Abu Hurayrah narrated that Allah's Messenger (ﷺ) said,

> *"Whoever has wronged a Muslim brother regarding his honour or his wealth, should make amends before the Day of Judgment, when neither dirham nor dīnār will be accepted; if he has righteous deeds, it will be taken from them, and if he doesn't have righteous deeds, it will be*

[27] Bukhari (Arabic-English), vol. 7, p. 390, hadith no. 575, Muslim (English trans), vol. 4, p. 1411 hadith nos. 6480 & 6485, *Sunan Abi Dāwūd*, vol. 2, p. 884, hadith no. 3102, and *Mishkāt al-Maṣābīḥ*, vol. 1, p. 333.

> *taken from the other's bad deeds and put on his (scale).*"[28]

If those dying are unable to repay their debts, they should, at least, have the sincere intention to do so and should inform their relatives about their debts. Either one of their relatives will repay their debts after their death, or the Prophet (ﷺ) will take responsibility for the debts. The Prophet (ﷺ) established the basic principle of divine accounting that if a person intends to do a good deed but is unable, he is rewarded by Allah for his intention. Consequently, he (ﷺ) is reported to have said in a *hadith qudsi*:

((اَلدَّينُ دَيْنَانِ ، فَمَنْ مَاتَ وَهُوَ يَنْوِي قَضَاءَهُ فأنَا وَلِيُّهُ ، وَمَنْ مَاتَ لاَ يَنْوِي قَضَاءَهُ، فَذَاكَ الَّذِي يُؤْخَذُ مَنْ حَسَنَاتِهِ، لَيْسَ يَوْمَئِذٍ دِينَار وَلاَ دِرْهَم)).

> *"There are two types of debt: whoever dies intending to repay it, I will be responsible for it, and whoever dies with no intention of repaying it, will have it taken from his good deeds. There will not be any dīnārs or dirhams on that Day.*"[29]

9) *Waṣiyyah* (Will)

Before dying, everyone leaving behind wealth and property should write or dictate a will in which they may give away up to one-third of their wealth to those who would not inherit from them based on the Islamic inheritance laws. This recommendation was instituted by Allah to protect the rights of non-inheriting relatives

---

[28] Bukhari (Arabic-English), vol. 3, p. 377, hadith no. 629, and *Mishkāt al-Maṣābīḥ*, vol. 2, p. 1062.

[29] Collected by Ṭabarani and authenticated in *Aḥkām al-Janā'iz*, p. 5.

and friends. Consequently, the Prophet (ﷺ) encouraged Muslims to write a will and keep it with them, as soon as the need arises.

عَنْ عَبْدِ اللَّهِ بْنِ عُمَرَ رَضِي اللَّهُ عَنهُمَا أَنَّ رَسُولَ اللَّه ﷺ قَالَ: ((مَا حَق امْرِئٍ مُسْلِمٍ لَهُ شَيء يُوصِي فِيهِ يَبِيتُ لَيْلَتَيْنِ إلاَّ وَوَصِيَّتُه مَكْتُوبَة عِنْدَهُ)).

'Abdullah ibn 'Umar related that the Messenger of Allah (ﷺ) said,

> *"It is not right for a Muslim who has something to bequeath to pass two nights without having it in writing in his possession."*[30]

Based on the principle of *waṣiyyah*, Muslims may write a will leaving, a maximum of one-third of their wealth for non-Muslims or receive in a will wealth from dead non-Muslim relatives. According to Islamic law, wealth obtained by *waṣiyyah* is not considered inheritance, but a gift. Islam considers 'inheritance' to be the portions of the deceased person's wealth which the law assigns to various family members in the absence of a will. According to the system of Islamic inheritance laws (*farā'iḍ*), non-Muslims are not classified as heirs to Muslims. Likewise, Muslims have no right to take portions of their dead non-Muslim relatives' wealth allotted by non-Islamic systems of inheritance. That is, if the deceased non-Muslim relative does not write a will and the non-Muslim state divides up his/her wealth according to its man-made laws, the Muslim relative is prohibited by Islamic

---

[30] Reported by Ibn 'Umar and collected in all of the six major books of hadith. See Bukhari (Arabic-English), vol. 4, p. 1, hadith no. 1, Muslim (English trans), vol. 3, p. 863, ḥadith no. 3987, *Sunan Abi Dāwūd*, vol. 2, p. 805, hadith no. 2856, *Mishkāt al-Maṣābīḥ*, vol. 1, p. 656, and *Muwaṭṭa Imām Mālik*, p. 329, hadith no. 1449.

law to accept any share allotted to him/her by that process.[31] The Prophet (ﷺ) is reported by Usāmah ibn Zayd to have said,

((لاَ يَرِثُ الْمُسْلِمُ الْكَافِرَ وَلاَ الْكَافِرُ الْمُسْلِمَ)).

"A Muslim must not inherit from a disbeliever, nor should a disbeliever inherit from a Muslim."[32]

---

[31] The fact that Western legal systems consider both willed wealth and state divided wealth to be 'inheritance' does not affect the Islamic distinction between the two.

[32] Bukhari (Arabic-English), vol. 8, p. 498, hadith no. 756, and Muslim (English trans), vol. 3, p. 852, hadith no. 3928.

CHAPTER 2: AFTER DEATH

A. Obligatory Actions on Those Present

Once the person expires, the relatives and those present are obliged to perform particular services for him or her.

1) Closing the Eyes and *Du'ā* (Supplication)

The eyes of the dead person should be closed and some prayers should be made for him, based on the following hadith of Umm Salamah:

عَنْ أُمِّ سَلَمَةَ قَالَتْ: دَخَلَ رَسُولُ اللَّهِ ﷺ عَلَي أَبِي سَلَمَةَ وَقَدْ شَقَّ بَصَرُهُ فَأَغْمَضَهُ ثُمَّ قَالَ: ((إِنَّ الرُّوحَ إِذَا قُبِضَ تَبِعَهُ الْبَصَرُ)). فَضَجَّ نَاس مِن أَهْلِهِ ، فَقَالَ: ((لاَ تَدْعُوا عَلَى أَنْفُسِكُمْ إِلاَّ بِخَيْرٍ، فَإِنَّ الْمَلاَئِكَةَ يُؤَمِّنُونَ عَلَى مَا تَقُولُونَ)). ثُمَّ قَالَ:

Umm Salamah said: "Allah's Messenger (Blessings and Peace be upon him) came in and found Abu Salamah's eyes wide open. He closed them and said, "*Indeed when the soul is snatched, the eyes follow it.*" Some people from his family began to scream, so he said, "*Only pray for good for yourselves, for verily the angels say 'Āmīn (so be it)', to whatever you say,*" He then prayed, saying,

((اللَّهُمَّ اغفِرْ لِأَبِي سَلَمَةَ وَارفَعْ دَرَجَتَهُ فِي الْمَهْدِيِّينَ وَاخْلُفْهُ فِي عَقِبِهِ فِي الْغَابِرِينَ وَاغْفِرْ لَنَا وَلَهُ يَا رَبَّ الْعَالَمِينَ وَافْسَحْ لَهُ فِي قَبْرِهِ وَنَوِّرْ لَهُ فِيهِ)).

"*Allahummagh-fir li Abi Salamah warfa' darajatahū fil-mahdīyīn* (O Allah, forgive Abu Salamah and raise his level among the rightly guided,) *wakhlufhu fi 'aqibihī filghābirīn* (and let his remaining offspring be like him.)" *waghfir lanā walahū yā Rabbal-'Ālamīn* (Forgive us and forgive him, O Lord of all the worlds) *wafsaḥ lahū fi qabrihī wa nawwir lahū fih* (and expand his grave and illuminate it for him.)[1]

2) Covering the Body

A sheet of cloth large enough to cover the whole body of the deceased should be drawn over the body. This was the approved practice of the Prophet (ﷺ) and the recorded practice of his Companions. For example:

عَنْ جَابِرٍ [قَالَ]: جِيءَ بِأَبِي يَوْمَ أُحُدٍ وَقَدْ مُثِّلَ بِهِ فَوُضِعَ بَيْنَ يَدَيْ رَسُولِ اللَّهِ ﷺ وَقَدْ سُجِّيَ بِثَوْبٍ فَجَعَلْتُ أُرِيدُ أَنْ أَكْشِفَ عَنْهُ فَنَهَانِي قَوْمِي فَأَمَرَ بِهِ النَّبِيُّ ﷺ فَرُفِعَ فَلَمَّا رُفِعَ سَمِعَ صَوْتَ بَاكِيَةٍ فَقَالَ: ((مَنْ هَذِهِ))؟ فَقَالُوا هَذِهِ بِنْتُ عَمْرٍو أَوْ أُخْتُ عَمْرٍو قَالَ: ((فَلَا تَبْكِ)) - أَوْ ((فَلِمَ تَبْكِي؟ مَا زَالَتِ الْمَلَائِكَةُ تُظِلُّهُ بِأَجْنِحَتِهَا حَتَّى رُفِعَ)).

Jābir said, "After the Battle of Uḥud, my father — who had been mutilated — was brought and placed in front of the Messenger of

[1] Muslim (English trans), vol. 2, Pp. 436-7, hadith no. 2003, *Sunan Abi Dāwūd*, vol. 2, p. 888, hadith no. 3112, *Sunan Ibn Mājah*, vol. 2, Pp. 370-1, hadith no. 1455, and *Mishkāt al-Maṣābīḥ*, vol. 1, p. 337.

Allah (ﷺ). He was covered in a cloth, and I wanted to uncover him, but the people forbade me. The Prophet (ﷺ) instructed that he should be uncovered, and when the cloth was lifted, he heard the voice of a woman crying. He asked, "Who is that?" They replied that she was 'Amr's daughter or sister, and he said,

> *"Don't cry, for the angels were shading him with their wings until (his soul) was lifted up."*[2]

عَنْ عَائِشَةَ النَّبِيِّ ﷺ سُجِّيَ فِي ثَوْبِ حِبَرَةٍ.

'Ā'ishah narrated that a striped Yemeni cloak[3] was drawn over the Prophet's body (when he died).[4]

In the case of a man who dies in a state of *iḥrām*[5] during Ḥajj or 'Umrah, neither the head nor face should be covered by a cloth. On the other hand, women, whose heads must be covered by the *iḥrām* garments but not their faces, would be treated accordingly.[6]

---

[2] *Ṣaḥīḥ Sunan an-Nasā'i*, vol. 2, p. 397, hadith no. 1738.

[3] *Ṣaḥīḥ Sunan Abi Dāwūd*, vol. 2, p. 766, note 1: The style of cloak called *hibarah* had green stripes and was made of cotton from Yemen.

[4] Bukhari (Arabic-English), vol. 2, Pp. 188-9, hadith no. 333, Muslim (English trans), vol. 2, p. 447, hadith nos. 2053 and 2056, *Sunan Abi Dāwūd*, vol. 2, p. 888, hadith no. 3114, and *Mishkāt al-Maṣābīḥ*, vol. 1, p. 337. Muslim's version explains that they later removed it and replaced it with three pieces of white cloth.

[5] *Iḥrām* represents the consecrated state of one who has made the intention for either the greater or lesser pilgrimage — Ḥajj or 'Umrah and has put on the specified garments, consisting of a cloak and a waist-wrapper. Men are not allowed to cover their heads when in this consecrated state.

[6] Ibn Ḥazm added that it was permissible to drape some material from the top of her head over her face as long as it was not in the form of the *niqāb*-style veil. He also stated that if either the male or female in *iḥrām* died after sunrise on the 10th of Dhul-Hijjah, they should be treated like a normal dead person, whether the deceased had completed the rites of *ramy* (i.e., stoning) or not. (*Al-Muḥallā*, vol. 5, p. 148, case 590.)

عَنِ ابْنِ عَبَّاسٍ رَضِي اللَّهُ عَنْهُمَا قَالَ: بَيْنَمَا رَجُلٌ وَاقِفٌ بِعَرَفَةَ إِذْ وَقَعَ عَنْ رَاحِلَتِهِ فَوَقَصَتْهُ (أَوْ قَالَ: فَأَوْقَصَتْهُ). قَالَ النَّبِيُّ ﷺ: ((اغْسِلُوهُ بِمَاءٍ وَسِدْرٍ وَكَفِّنُوهُ فِي ثَوْبَيْنِ وَلاَ تُحَنِّطُوهُ وَلاَ تُخَمِّرُوا رَأْسَهُ فَإِنَّهُ يُبْعَثُ يَوْمَ الْقِيَامَةِ مُلَبِّيًا)).

Ibn 'Abbās stated, "While a man was standing at 'Arafah, he fell off his horse and it trampled him to death. The Prophet (ﷺ) said,

> *"Wash him with water and lote-tree leaves, wrap him in his two sheets of cloth, but do not put perfumed oil on him, nor cover his head and face, for verily Allah will resurrect him on the Day of Resurrection making talbīyah*[7]'."[8]

3) Hastening the Burial

Once death is evident, the body should be prepared and taken out of the house for prayer and burial as soon as possible. In this way, contact with the dead body is minimized, which keeps the grief and hurt of seeing the dead down to a minimum. Abu Hurayrah related that the Prophet (ﷺ) said,

((أَسْرِعُوا بِالْجِنَازَةِ)).

"Hasten the funeral rites."[9]

---

[7] *Talbīyah* is the supplication repeated aloud by pilgrims at the beginning of 'Umrah or Ḥajj and during their journey to Makkah.

[8] Bukhari (Arabic-English), vol. 2, Pp. 199-200, hadith nos. 355-357, Muslim (English trans), vol. 2, Pp. 596-7, hadith nos. 2747 & 2750, and *Sunan Abi Dāwūd*, vol. 2, p. 920, hadith no. 3232.

[9] Collected in all of the six major books of hadith. See Bukhari (Arabic-English), vol. 2, p. 225, hadith no. 401, Muslim (English trans), vol. 2, p. 448, hadith no. 2059, *Sunan Abi Dāwūd*, vol. 2, Pp. 897-8, hadith no. 3153, *Sunan Ibn Mājah*, vol. 2, p. 382, hadith no. 1477, and *Mishkāt al-Maṣābīḥ*, vol. 1, p. 338.

Consequently, it is not permissible for Muslims to delay the burial in order for the maximum number of relatives to see the deceased, as is common practice among other communities. The custom of delaying funerals created the need for embalming in order to slow down the decaying process.

4) Location of Burial

The dead should be buried in the same area where they died. Transporting the body to another area or another country is not permissible, because it contradicts the Prophet's order to hasten the burial and it also necessitates unnecessary additional expenses. Furthermore, the Prophet (ﷺ) specifically forbade his followers from transferring bodies from the locality in which they died.

عَنْ جَابِرِ بْنِ عَبْدِ اللَّهِ قَالَ: كُنَّا حَمَلْنَا الْقَتْلَى يَوْمَ أُحُدٍ لِنَدْفِنَهُمْ فَجَاءَ مُنَادِي النَّبِيِّ ﷺ فَقَالَ: إِنَّ رَسُولَ اللَّهِ ﷺ يَأْمُرُكُمْ أَنْ تَدْفِنُوا الْقَتْلَى فِي مَضَاجِعِهِمْ فَرَدَدْنَاهُمْ.

Jābir ibn 'Abdillah said, "On the day of the Battle of Uḥud,[10] the dead were being carried (back to Madīnah) for burial in al-Baqi',[11] when the Prophet's announcer called out, "Allah's Messenger orders you to bury the dead where they lie." This (announcement came) after my mother had already tied my father and uncle to the sides of her camel in order to bury them in al-Baqi'. However, she returned them to where they were killed (for burial)."[12]

---

[10] Uḥud is a volcanic hill with a plain stretching before it on the western outskirts of Madīnah. The Quraysh defeated the Muslims there in the third year of the Hijrah (625 CE). (*The Concise Encyclopaedia of Islam*, p. 68).

[11] The name given to the graveyard of the city of Madīnah.

[12] Collected in the Four *Sunans*. See *Sunan Abi Dāwūd*, vol. 2, p. 899, hadith no. 3159, *Sunan Ibn Mājah*, vol. 2, Pp. 403-4, hadith no. 1516, and *Mishkāt al-*

Imām an-Nawawi in his book, *al-Adhkār*, said, "If (the dying person) requests or writes in his will that his body be transported to another country, it should be disregarded, since transporting the dead to another locality is *ḥarām*, according to the authentic position held by most scholars."[13]

5) Debts

All outstanding debts of the dead person should be repaid from the wealth that he or she left behind, even if it consumes all of the inheritance. If the dead person was without wealth or the inheritance was not sufficient to cover all of his or her debts, the Islamic state will be responsible to repay the remainder, if the dead person had made serious efforts to pay it. 'Ā'ishah quoted the Prophet (ﷺ) as saying,

((مَنْ حَمَلَ مِنْ أُمَّتِي دَيْنًا ثُمَّ جَهَدَ فِي قَضَائِهِ ثُمَّ مَاتَ قَبْلَ أَنْ يَقْضِيَهُ فَأَنَا وَلِيُّهُ)).

> *"Whoever among my Ummah has a debt and strives to repay it, but dies (before being able to do so), I will be responsible for it."*[14]

Allah identified the *ghārimūn* (debtors) as being among those eligible to receive *zakāh*. If, however, the state was unable to repay the dead person's debts, any Muslim may voluntarily repay the debts as an act of charity.

Maṣābīḥ, vol. 1, p. 356. It is authenticated by Shaykh al-Albāni in *Ṣaḥīḥ Sunan Abi Dāwūd*, vol. 2, p. 610, hadith no. 2710, and in *Aḥkām al-Janā'iz*, p. 14.

[13] *Ṣaḥīḥ Kitāb al-Adhkār*, vol. 1, p. 433.

[14] Collected in *Musnad Aḥmad*, vol. 6, p. 74, and authenticated in *Aḥkām al-Janā'iz*, p. 19.

عَنْ سَعْدِ بْنِ الأَطْوَلِ قَالَ: مَاتَ أَخِي وَتَرَكَ ثَلاثَ مِائَةِ دِينَارٍ وَتَرَكَ وَلَدًا صِغَارًا فَأَرَدْتُ أَنْ أُنْفِقَ عَلَيْهِمْ، فَقَالَ لِي رَسُولُ اللَّهِ ﷺ: ((إِنَّ أَخَاكَ مَحْبُوسٌ بِدَيْنِهِ فَاذْهَبْ فَاقْضِ عَنْهُ)). قَالَ: فَذَهَبْتُ فَقَضَيْتُ عَنْهُ ثُمَّ جِئْتُ فَقُلْتُ يَا رَسُولَ اللَّهِ قَدْ قَضَيْتُ عَنْهُ وَلَمْ يَبْقَ إِلاَّ امْرَأَةٌ تَدَّعِي دِينَارَيْنِ وَلَيْسَتْ لَهَا بَيِّنَةٌ. قَالَ: ((أَعْطِهَا فَإِنَّهَا صَادِقَةٌ)).

Sa‘d ibn al-Aṭwal narrated that his brother died and left behind three hundred dirhams and a family, and he (Sa‘d) wanted to spend it on his brother's family. However, the Prophet (ﷺ) informed him, "*Certainly, your brother is imprisoned by his debt, so go and pay it off.*" Sa‘d went and paid it off, then came to the Prophet (ﷺ) and said, "I have paid it all off except for two *dīnārs* claimed by a woman who does not have any proof." The Prophet (ﷺ) told him, "*Give it to her, for indeed she is truthful.*"[15]

B. Permissible Actions by Those Present

1) Uncovering the Face and Kissing it

Those present at the individual's death or those who come to see the dead person for the last time are allowed to uncover the face and kiss it. Kissing the face of the dead is considered part of the Sunnah of the Prophet (ﷺ) and his Companions.

عَنْ عَائِشَةَ قَالَتْ رَأَيْتُ رَسُولَ اللَّهِ ﷺ يُقَبِّلُ عُثْمَانَ بْنَ مَظْعُونٍ وَهُوَ مَيِّتٌ حَتَّى رَأَيْتُ الدُّمُوعَ تَسِيلُ.

---

[15] Collected in *Musnad Aḥmad*, vol. 4, p. 136, and authenticated by Shaykh al-Albāni in *Ṣaḥīḥ Sunan Ibn Mājah*, vol. 2, p. 57, hadith no. 1973, and *Aḥkām al-Janā'iz*, p. 15, For the English text, see *Mishkāt al-Maṣābīḥ*, vol. 1, p. 626.

'Ā'ishah stated, "I saw Allah's Messenger kiss 'Uthmān ibn Math'ūn after he had died and I saw his tears flow.[16]"

عنْ عَائِشَةَ رَضِي اللَّهُ عَنْهَا زَوْجَ النَّبِيِّ ﷺ : أَقْبَلَ أَبُو بَكْرٍ رضي الله عنه عَلَى فَرَسِهِ مِنْ مَسْكَنِهِ بِالسُّنْحِ حَتَّى نَزَلَ فَدَخَلَ الْمَسْجِدَ فَلَمْ يُكَلِّمِ النَّاسَ حَتَّى دَخَلَ عَلَى عَائِشَةَ رَضِي اللَّهُ عَنْهَا فَتَيَمَّمَ النَّبِيَّ ﷺ وَهُوَ مُسَجًّى بِبُرْدِ حِبَرَةٍ فَكَشَفَ عَنْ وَجْهِهِ ثُمَّ أَكَبَّ عَلَيْهِ فَقَبَّلَهُ ثُمَّ بَكَى.

'Ā'ishah also said, "Abu Bakr came riding on his horse from his home in *Sunḥ*. He dismounted and entered the masjid without saying anything to the people until he entered 'Ā'ishah's house. He went to the Prophet, who was covered in his striped Yemeni cloak, uncovered his face, bent over and kissed him (between his eyes)[17] and cried."[18]

2) Crying

Those present and the relatives of the deceased are allowed to cry for a maximum period of three days.

عَنْ عَبْدِ اللَّهِ بْنِ جَعْفَرٍ أَنَّ النَّبِيَّ ﷺ أَمْهَلَ آلَ جَعْفَرٍ ثَلَاثًا أَنْ يَأْتِيَهُمْ ، ثُمَّ أَتَاهُمْ فَقَالَ: ((لاَ تَبْكُوا عَلَى أَخِي بَعْدَ الْيَوْمِ)).

'Abdullah ibn Ja'far narrated that the Prophet delayed coming to

---

[16] *Sunan Abi Dāwūd* vol. 2, p. 898, hadith no. 3157, *Sunan Ibn Mājah* vol. 2, p. 371 hadith no. 1456, and *Mishkāt al-Maṣābīḥ*, vol. 1, p. 338, and authenticated by Shaykh al-Albani in *Ṣaḥīḥ Sunan Ibn Mājah*, vol. 2, p. 246, hadith no. 1191.

[17] This addition is found in *Ṣaḥīḥ Sunan an-Nasā'i*, vol. 2, p. 396, hadith no. 1735.

[18] Bukhari (Arabic-English), vol. 2, p. 188, hadith no. 333. the colour of the cloak was green see footnote 37.

visit Ja'far's family for three days after his death, then he came to them and said, "*Do not cry for my brother after today.*"[19]

In the previously mentioned hadith of 'Ā'ishah concerning 'Uthmān ibn Madh'ūn, she stated that the Prophet (ﷺ) cried until tears overflowed from his eyelids.

عَنْ أَنَسِ بْنِ مَالِكٍ ﷺ قَالَ: دَخَلْنَا مَعَ رَسُولِ اللَّهِ ﷺ عَلَى أَبِي سَيْفٍ الْقَيْنِ وَكَانَ ظِئْرًا لإِبْرَاهِيمَ عَلَيْهِ السَّلاَم فَأَخَذَ رَسُولُ اللَّهِ ﷺ إِبْرَاهِيمَ فَقَبَّلَهُ وَشَمَّهُ ثُمَّ دَخَلْنَا عَلَيْهِ بَعْدَ ذَلِكَ وَإِبْرَاهِيمُ يَجُودُ بِنَفْسِهِ فَجَعَلَتْ عَيْنَا رَسُولِ اللَّهِ ﷺ تَذْرِفَانِ فَقَالَ لَهُ عَبْدُالرَّحْمَنِ بْنُ عَوْفٍ ﷺ وَأَنْتَ يَا رَسُولَ اللَّهِ؟ فَقَالَ: ((يَا ابْنَ عَوْفٍ إِنَّهَا رَحْمَةٌ)). ثُمَّ أَتْبَعَهَا بِأُخْرَى فَقَالَ ﷺ: ((إِنَّ الْعَيْنَ تَدْمَعُ وَالْقَلْبَ يَحْزَنُ وَلاَ نَقُولُ إِلاَّ مَا يَرْضَى رَبُّنَا وَإِنَّا بِفِرَاقِكَ يَا إِبْرَاهِيمُ لَمَحْزُونُونَ)).

Anas ibn Mālik reported that they went with the Prophet (ﷺ) to visit Abu Sayf, the husband of Ibrāhīm's[20] wet nurse, and the Prophet (ﷺ) took Ibrāhīm, cuddled him and kissed him. When they returned later to visit him, Ibrāhīm was breathing his last and the Prophet's eyes welled up with tears. 'Abdur-Raḥmān ibn 'Awf asked, "Even you, O Messenger of Allah?" The Prophet (ﷺ) replied, "*O son of 'Awf, verily, it is a mercy.*" His eyes again were filled with tears and he (ﷺ) said, "*Verily the eyes fill with tears and the heart feels sorrow, but we only say that which pleases our Lord. Indeed, we are sorrowful at your parting, O Ibrāhīm.*"[21]

---

[19] *Sunan Abi Dāwūd*, vol. 3, p. 1165, hadith no. 4180, and *Mishkāt al-Maṣābīḥ*, vol. 2, p. 934, and authenticated by Shaykh al-Albāni in *Ṣaḥīḥ Sunan Abi Dāwūd*, vol. 2, p. 790, hadith no. 3532.

[20] Ibrāhīm was the Prophet's son by his Egyptian Coptic wife, Mariah.

[21] Bukhari (Arabic-English), vol. 2, Pp. 219-20, hadith no. 390, Muslim (English trans), vol. 4, p. 1243, hadith no. 5733, *Sunan Abi Dāwūd*, vol. 2,=

3. Patience

Relatives of the deceased are obliged to be patient, practice self restraint, and gracefully accept Allah's decree, because Allah has already promised mankind that He would test them.

﴿وَلَنَبْلُوَنَّكُم بِشَىْءٍ مِّنَ ٱلْخَوْفِ وَٱلْجُوعِ وَنَقْصٍ مِّنَ ٱلْأَمْوَٰلِ وَٱلْأَنفُسِ وَٱلثَّمَرَٰتِ ۗ وَبَشِّرِ ٱلصَّٰبِرِينَ ﴿١٥٥﴾﴾ (سورة البقرة ٢: ١٥٥)

﴿Verily I[22] will test you with fear and hunger, and loss of wealth, life and the fruit [of your labour], so give glad tidings to the patient ones.﴾ (Qur'an 2: 155)

Among the glad tidings for those who are patient when loved ones are lost is that a home is prepared for them in Paradise. Abu Mūsā al-Ash'ari quoted Allah's Messenger (ﷺ) as saying,

((إِذَا مَاتَ وَلَدُ الْعَبْدِ قَالَ اللَّهُ لِمَلَائِكَتِهِ: قَبَضْتُمْ وَلَدَ عَبْدِي. فَيَقُولُونَ: نَعَمْ. فَيَقُولُ: قَبَضْتُمْ ثَمَرَةَ فُؤَادِهِ. فَيَقُولُونَ: نَعَمْ. فَيَقُولُ: مَاذَا قَالَ عَبْدِي؟ فَيَقُولُونَ: حَمِدَكَ وَاسْتَرْجَعَ. فَيَقُولُ اللَّهُ: ابْنُوا لِعَبْدِي بَيْتًا فِي الْجَنَّةِ وَسَمُّوهُ بَيْتَ الْحَمْدِ)).

"If a child of (Allah's) slave dies, Allah will say to His angels, "You took My slave's child." They will reply, "Yes." He will then say, "You took the love of his life,"[23] and they will reply, "Yes." He will then ask, "What did My slave say?" And they will reply, "He praised you and

=p. 891 hadith no. 3120, *Sunan Ibn Mājah*, vol. 2, p. 442, hadith no. 1589 (on the authority of Asmā' bint Yazīd) and *Mishkāt al-Maṣābīḥ*, vol. 1, p. 360.

22 Literally, "we"; known in English as the "majestic we" or the "royal we" used by those of great importance.

23 Literally, "the fruit of his heart."

said, "Surely, we belong to Allah and to Him we will return." Allah will then say, "Build a house in Paradise for My slave and call it the House of Praise."[24]

However, true patience for which Allah promises reward is that which is practiced when the calamity first strikes. The real test of patience is at the time of the calamity. Being patient after the initial shock and reaction have worn off is not considered real patience.

عَنْ أَنَسِ بْنِ مَالِكٍ ﷺ قَالَ: مَرَّ النَّبِيُّ ﷺ بِامْرَأَةٍ تَبْكِي عِنْدَ قَبْرٍ فَقَالَ: ((اتَّقِي اللَّهَ وَاصْبِرِي)). قَالَتْ: إِلَيْكَ عَنِّي، فَإِنَّكَ لَمْ تُصَبْ بِمُصِيبَتِي وَلَمْ تَعْرِفْهُ فَقِيلَ لَهَا: إِنَّهُ النَّبِيُّ ﷺ فَأَتَتْ بَابَ النَّبِيِّ ﷺ فَلَمْ تَجِدْ عِنْدَهُ بَوَّابِينَ فَقَالَتْ: لَمْ أَعْرِفْكَ. فَقَالَ: ((إِنَّمَا الصَّبْرُ عِنْدَ الصَّدْمَةِ الأُولَى)).

Anas ibn Mālik narrated that once the Prophet (ﷺ) passed by a woman crying beside a grave and said to her, "*Fear Allah and be patient.*" She replied, "Get away from me, for you haven't been afflicted with my misfortune, and you don't even know what it is!" Someone informed her that it was the Prophet (ﷺ) (and the news struck her like death).[25] She ran to the Prophet's door — where she did not find any guard and called out, "O Messenger of Allah, verily I didn't know it was you." The Prophet (ﷺ) replied, "*True patience is with the first shock.*"[26]

---

[24] *Ṣaḥīḥ Sunan at-Tirmidhi*, vol. 1, Pp. 298-9, hadith no. 814.

[25] This addition is in the narration of *Ṣaḥīḥ Muslim*.

[26] Bukhari (Arabic-English) vol. 2, p. 208, hadith no. 372, Muslim (English trans), vol. 2, p. 439, hadith no. 2013, *Sunan Abi Dāwūd*, vol. 2, p. 890 hadith no. 3118, *Sunan Ibn Mājah*, vol. 2, p. 446, hadith no. 1596, and *Mishkāt al-Maṣābīḥ*, vol. 1, p. 361. The wording is from *Sunan Ibn Mājah*, vol. 2, p. 452, hadith no. 1605.

Patience and self restraint at the death of children have especially great rewards because of the severity of their death on their parents. Abu Hurayrah reported that the Prophet (ﷺ) said,

((مَا مِنْ مُسْلِمَيْنِ يَمُوتُ بَيْنَهُمَا ثَلاَثَةُ أَوْلاَدٍ لَمْ يَبْلُغُوا الْحِنْثَ إِلاَّ أَدْخَلَهُمَا اللَّهُ بِفَضْلِ رَحْمَتِهِ إِيَّاهُمُ الْجَنَّةَ))، قَالَ: ((يُقَالُ لَهُمُ ادْخُلُوا الْجَنَّةَ فَيَقُولُونَ: حَتَّى يَدْخُلَ آبَاؤُنَا. فَيُقَالُ: ادْخُلُوا الْجَنَّةَ أَنْتُمْ وَآبَاؤُكُمْ)).

> *"If any Muslim couple has three of their children die before reaching maturity, Allah will enter them into Paradise along with their children, out of His mercy.*[27] *The children will wait at the gates of Paradise. When they are told to enter, they will reply, "Not until our two parents come." They will be told to enter Paradise along with their parents by Allah's mercy."*[28]

عَنْ أَبِي حَسَّانَ قَالَ: قُلْتُ لِأَبِي هُرَيْرَةَ إِنَّهُ قَدْ مَاتَ لِيَ ابْنَانِ فَمَا أَنْتَ مُحَدِّثِي عَنْ رَسُولِ اللَّهِ ﷺ بِحَدِيثٍ تُطَيِّبُ بِهِ أَنْفُسَنَا عَنْ مَوْتَانَا. قَالَ: قَالَ نَعَمْ. ((صِغَارُهُمْ دَعَامِيصُ الْجَنَّةِ يَتَلَقَّى أَحَدُهُمْ أَبَاهُ)) - أَوْ قَالَ: ((أَبَوَيْهِ)) - ((فَيَأْخُذُ بِثَوْبِهِ)) - أَوْ قَالَ بِيَدِهِ كَمَا آخُذُ أَنَا بِصَنِفَةِ ثَوْبِكَ هَذَا - ((فَلاَ يَتَنَاهَى)) - أَوْ قَالَ: ((فَلاَ يَنْتَهِي حَتَّى يُدْخِلَهُ اللَّهُ وَأَبَاهُ الْجَنَّةَ)).

Abu Ḥassān related, "I told Abu Hurayrah that my two children had died (and asked him to) narrate to me any hadith from Allah's Messenger (ﷺ) which would soothe our hearts in our

[27] Bukhari (Arabic-English), vol. 2, Pp. 192-3, hadith nos. 340-2, Muslim (English trans), vol. 4, Pp. 1384-5, hadith nos. 6365 & 6368.

[28] *Ṣaḥīḥ Sunan an-Nasā'i* vol. 2, p. 405, hadith no. 1770.

bereavement." He replied, "*Yes. Small children are the tadpoles of Paradise. If one of them meets his father,*[29] *he would grab his garment,*[30] *and he will not remove his hand from it until Allah causes his father to enter Paradise.*"[31]

Allah has promised a special additional reward for any woman who loses three children, because she suffers even more than her husband when a child dies. It is she who carries the child within her for nine months, gives birth to him, nurses him, etc. If she is patient, she will be granted as even greater reward than her spouse.

عَنْ أَبِي سَعِيدٍ الْخُدْرِيِّ أَنَّ النِّسَاء قُلْنَ: غَلَبَنَا عَلَيْكَ الرِّجَالُ يَا رَسُولَ اللَّهِ، فَاجْعَلْ لَنَا يَوْمًا، يَا رَسُولَ اللَّهِ، نَأْتِيكَ فِيهِ. فَوَاعَدَهُنَّ مِيعَادًا، فَأَمَرَ هُنَّ وَوَعَظَهُنَّ وَقَالَ: ((مَا مِنْكُنَّ امْرَأَةٌ يَمُوتُ لَهَا ثَلاثَةٌ مِنَ الْوَلَدِ إِلاَّ كَانُوا لَهَا حِجَابًا مِنَ النَّارِ)). فَقَالَتِ امْرَأَةٌ: أَو اثْنَانِ؟ فَإِنَّهُ مَاتَ لِي اثْنَانِ. فَقَالَ رَسُولُ اللَّهِ ﷺ: ((أَوِ اثْنَانِ)).

Abu Sa'īd al-Khudri mentioned that the women said to the Messenger of Allah, "O Messenger of Allah, the men are getting more of your time than we are. Please set aside a day just for us when we can come to you." He promised them an appointed time. (On that day,) he instructed them and advised them. One of the things he said was, "*Any woman who has three children that die before her will be shielded by them from the Hellfire.*" A woman asked, "What about two children, for I have had two die?" He

29 The narrator added, "or he said: his parents."

30 The narrator added, "or he demonstrated with his hand, saying, 'The way I take hold of the hem of your garment.'"

31 Muslim (English trans), vol. 4, p. 1385, hadith no. 6370. Also reported by Aḥmad.

replied that would also shield her.[32]

4. *Al-Istirjā'*

When the news of death in the family reaches the relatives and friends, the first thing that they should say is the following Qur'anic verse:

﴿... إِنَّا لِلَّهِ وَإِنَّآ إِلَيْهِ رَٰجِعُونَ ﴿١٥٦﴾﴾ (سورة البقرة ٢ : ١٥٦)

﴿*...Innā lil-lāhi wa innā ilayhi rāji'ūn* [Verily we belong to Allah and verily to Him we must return.]﴾[33]

(Qur'an 2: 156)

In the case of the husband or wife, they should add, "*Allahumma ajirni fi musībati wakh-luf li khayran minhā* (O Allah grant me refuge in my affliction and replace me with something better.")

عَنْ أُمِّ سَلَمَةَ أَنَّهَا قَالَتْ : سَمِعْتُ رَسُولَ اللَّهِ ﷺ يَقُولُ : ((مَا مِنْ مُسْلِم تُصِيبُهُ مُصِيبَةٌ فَيَقُولُ مَا أَمَرَهُ اللَّهُ ﴿إِنَّا لِلَّهِ وَإِنَّا إِلَيْهِ رَاجِعُونَ﴾ اللَّهُمَّ أْجُرْنِي فِي مُصِيبَتِي وَأَخْلِفْ لِي خَيْرًا مِنْهَا إِلاَّ أَخْلَفَ اللَّهُ لَهُ خَيْرًا مِنْهَا)) . قَالَتْ فَلَمَّا مَاتَ أَبُو سَلَمَةَ قُلْتُ : أَيُّ الْمُسْلِمِينَ خَيْرٌ مِنْ أَبِي سَلَمَةَ ، أَوَّلُ بَيْتٍ هَاجَرَ إِلَى رَسُولِ اللَّهِ ﷺ ؟ ثُمَّ إِنِّي قُلْتُهَا ، فَأَخْلَفَ اللَّهُ لِي رَسُولَ اللَّهِ ﷺ . قَالَتْ : أَرْسَلَ إِلَيَّ رَسُولُ اللَّهِ ﷺ حَاطِبَ بْنَ أَبِي بَلْتَعَةَ يَخْطُبُنِي لَهُ ، فَقُلْتُ : إِنَّ لِي بِنْتًا وَأَنَا غَيُورٌ فَقَالَ : ((أَمَّا ابْنَتُهَا فَنَدْعُو اللَّهَ أَنْ يُغْنِيَهَا عَنْهَا وَأَدْعُو اللَّهَ أَنْ يَذْهَبَ بِالْغَيْرَةِ)) .

---

[32] Bukhari (Arabic-English), vol. 2, Pp. 192-93, hadith no. 341, Muslim (English trans), vol. 4, p. 1385, hadith no. 6368, *Mishkāt al-Maṣābīḥ*, vol. 1, p. 367, and *Muwaṭṭa*, p. 112, hadith no. 551.

[33] This *du'ā* is known in Arabic as *al-Istirjā'*.

Umm Salamah stated that Allah's Messenger (ﷺ) said, "*If any Muslim who is afflicted with a misfortune says: Innā lil-lāhi wa innā ilayhi rāji'ūn, Allahumma ajirni fi muṣībati wakh-luf li khayram minhā, Allah will replace it with something better.*" She then said,"When Abu Salamah died I asked myself, "Who among Muslims is better than Abu Salamah, the first family to make the *hijrah*?" When I said (the prayer), Allah replaced (Abu Salamah) with Allah's Messenger (ﷺ). Allah's Messenger (ﷺ) sent Ḥāṭib ibn Abi Balta'ah to propose to me (on his behalf). I said, "I have a daughter and I am very jealous." The Prophet (ﷺ) said, "*As for her daughter, we ask Allah to make her less dependent upon Umm Salamah, and I ask Allah to remove her jealousy.*"[34]

5. *Al-Ḥidād* (Mourning)

Women are required to avoid all forms of beautification as a sign of mourning for their husbands, children or relatives. This does not contradict the recommendations for patience, as long as the mourning does not exceed three days for her child or relative and four months and ten days for her husband.

عَنْ أُمِّ عَطِيَّةَ قَالَتْ: كُنَّا نُنْهَى أَنْ نُحِدَّ عَلَى مَيِّتٍ فَوْقَ ثَلاَثٍ إِلاَّ عَلَى زَوْجٍ، أَرْبَعَةَ أَشْهُرٍ وَعَشْرًا، وَلاَ نَكْتَحِلَ وَلاَ نَطَّيَّبَ وَلاَ نَلْبَسَ ثَوْبًا مَصْبُوغًا إِلاَّ ثَوْبَ عَصْبٍ. وَقَدْ رُخِّصَ لَنَا عِنْدَ الطُّهْرِ إِذَا اغْتَسَلَتْ إِحْدَانَا مِنْ مَحِيضِهَا فِي نُبْذَةٍ مِنْ كُسْتِ أَظْفَارٍ.

Umm 'Aṭīyah said, "We were forbidden to mourn for more than three days for a dead person, except for a husband, in which case a

[34] Muslim (English trans), vol. 2, Pp. 435-36, hadith no. 1999, *Sunan Abi Dāwūd*, vol. 2, p. 888, hadith no. 3113, *Sunan Ibn Mājah*, vol. 2, p. 447, hadith no. 1598, *Muwaṭṭa*, p. 112, hadith no. 554, and *Mishkāt al-Maṣābīḥ*, vol. 1, p. 337.

woman should mourn for four months and ten days. (During this period) we were not allowed to put *kohl* in our eyes, nor perfume ourselves, nor wear coloured clothes, except *'aṣab*[35] cloth. It was permissible for us at the time of bathing at the end of menses to use a small amount of incense."[36]

عَنْ أُمِّ سَلَمَةَ زَوْجِ النَّبِيِّ ﷺ عَنِ النَّبِيِّ ﷺ أَنَّهُ قَالَ: ((الْمُتَوَفَّى عَنْهَا زَوْجُهَا لاَ تَلْبَسُ الْمُعَصْفَرَ مِنَ الثِّيَابِ وَلاَ الْمُمَشَّقَةَ وَلاَ الْحُلِيَّ وَلاَ تَخْتَضِبُ وَلاَ تَكْتَحِلُ)).

The Prophet's wife, Umm Salamah, quoted him as saying,

> *"A widow must not wear clothes dyed yellow or red, nor wear ornaments, henna or kohl."*[37]

The mourning widow should spend her period of mourning in her husband's house, according to a number of authentic statements of the Prophet (ﷺ) as well as the consensus of early scholars.[38]

عَنْ زَيْنَبَ بِنْتِ كَعْبِ ابْنِ عَجْرَةَ أَنَّ الْفُرَيْعَةَ بِنْتَ مَالِكِ بْنِ سِنَانٍ – وَهِيَ أُخْتُ أَبِي سَعِيدٍ الْخُدْرِيِّ – أَخْبَرَتْهَا أَنَّهَا جَاءَتْ إِلَى رَسُولِ اللَّهِ ﷺ تَسْأَلُهُ أَنْ تَرْجِعَ إِلَى أَهْلِهَا فِي بَنِي خُدْرَةَ، فَإِنَّ زَوْجَهَا خَرَجَ فِي طَلَبِ أَعْبُدٍ لَهُ أَبَقُوا حَتَّى إِذَا كَانُوا بِطَرَفِ الْقَدُومِ لَحِقَهُمْ، فَقَتَلُوهُ، فَسَأَلْتُ رَسُولَ اللَّهِ ﷺ أَنْ أَرْجِعَ إِلَى أَهْلِي فَإِنِّي لَمْ يَتْرُكْنِي فِي مَسْكَنٍ

---

[35] Yemeni cloth made from partially dyed yarn. (*Arabic-English Lexicon*, vol. 2, p. 2058)

[36] Bukhari (Arabic-English), vol. 7, Pp. 193-4, hadith no. 254, and Muslim (English trans), vol. 2, p. 778, hadith no. 3552.

[37] *Sunan Abi Dāwūd*, vol. 2, p. 627, hadith no. 2297, and authenticated by Shaykh al-Albāni in *Ṣaḥīḥ Sunan Abi Dāwūd*, vol. 2, p. 438, hadith no. 2020.

[38] *Al-Mughni*, vol. 11, Pp. 290-1.

يَمْلِكُهُ وَلاَ نَفَقَةٍ. قَالَتْ: فَقَالَ رَسُولُ اللَّهِ ﷺ: ((نَعَمْ)). قَالَتْ: فَخَرَجْتُ حَتَّى إِذَا كُنْتُ فِي الْحُجْرَةِ أَوْ فِي الْمَسْجِدِ دَعَانِي أَوْ أَمَرَ بِي فَدُعِيتُ لَهُ فَقَالَ: ((كَيْفَ قُلْتِ))؟ فَرَدَدْتُ عَلَيْهِ الْقِصَّةَ الَّتِي ذَكَرْتُ مِنْ شَأْنِ زَوْجِي قَالَتْ فَقَالَ: ((امْكُثِي فِي بَيْتِكِ حَتَّى يَبْلُغَ الْكِتَابُ أَجَلَهُ)). قَالَتْ: فَاعْتَدَدْتُ فِيهِ أَرْبَعَةَ أَشْهُرٍ وَعَشْرًا. قَالَتْ: فَلَمَّا كَانَ عُثْمَانُ بْنُ عَفَّانَ أَرْسَلَ إِلَيَّ فَسَأَلَنِي عَنْ ذَلِكَ فَأَخْبَرْتُهُ فَاتَّبَعَهُ وَقَضَى بِهِ.

Zaynab bint Ka'b reported that Furay'ah bint Mālik[39] told her that she went to Allah's Messenger (ﷺ) and asked him permission to return to her family, the Khudrah clan, since her husband had been killed at *al-Qudūm* by some of his runaway slaves, whom he had gone after. She asked Allah's Messenger (ﷺ), "Can I return to my family, since he didn't leave me in a house owned by him, nor did he leave me any maintenance?" She reported that Allah's Messenger (ﷺ) said, "*Yes.*" She then said, "I left and when I reached the apartment or the masjid, he (ﷺ) called for me and asked, "*What did you say*?" I repeated the story to him and he said, "*Stay in your house until your term elapses.*" So I passed the waiting period of four months and ten days in it. When 'Uthmān ibn 'Affān became caliph, he sent an emissary to me and asked about this incident and I informed him. He accepted it and afterwards decided cases according to it."[40]

However, a widow may leave her home to fulfill her economic and social needs. For example, if she works to sustain her family, she may continue to leave her home daily for the period of her work.

---

[39] The sister of the famous Companion of the Prophet, Abu Sa'īd al-Khudri.

[40] *Sunan Abi Dāwūd*, vol. 2, p. 625, hadith no. 2293, and authenticated by Shaykh al-Albāni in *Ṣaḥīḥ Sunan Abi Dāwūd*, vol. 2, Pp. 436-7, hadith no. 2016.

عَنْ جَابِرٍ قَالَ: طُلِّقَتْ خَالَتِي ثَلاَثًا فَخَرَجَتْ تَجُدُّ نَخْلاً لَهَا فَلَقِيَهَا رَجُلٌ فَنَهَاهَا فَأَتَتِ النَّبِيَّ ﷺ فَذَكَرَتْ ذَلِكَ لَهُ فَقَالَ لَهَا: ((اخْرُجِي فَجُدِّي نَخْلَكِ لَعَلَّكِ أَنْ تَصَدَّقِي مِنْهُ أَوْ تَفْعَلِي خَيْرًا)).

Jābir said, "My maternal aunt was divorced after three pronouncements, and she went out to cut down fruit from her palm trees." A man met her and forbade her from going out. She went to the Prophet (ﷺ) and mentioned it to him and he said,

> *"Go out and cut down dates from your date-palms, that you may give some charity or do some other act of kindness."*[41]

Social visits to relatives and friends are also permissible, however, the widow should pass the night in her own home.[42] The famous student of the Prophet's Companions, Mujāhid, said that when some men were martyred in the Battle of Uḥud, their widows went to the Messenger of Allah (ﷺ) and said, "O Messenger of Allah, we feel lonely during the nights. Could we pass the night at each other's homes and return to our own homes in the early morning?" The Messenger of Allah (ﷺ) replied,

> *"Chat among yourselves until you wish to go to sleep. Then each one should return to her own home."*[43]

---

[41] *Sunan Abi Dāwūd*, vol. 2, p. 623, hadith no. 2290, and authenticated by Shaykh al-Albāni in *Ṣaḥīḥ Sunan Abi Dāwūd*, vol. 2, p. 435, hadith no. 2011.

[42] *Al-Mughni*, vol. 11, p. 297.

[43] Collected by al-Bayhaqi in *as-Sunan al-Kubrā*, vol. 7, hadith no. 436, and by 'Abdur-Razzāq in *al-Muṣnannaf*, vol. 7, hadith no. 37. The hadith is *mursal*, because Mujāhid didn't say from whom he heard it. Scholars of *fiqh*, such as Imām Mālik and Imām Abu Ḥanīfah, have tended to support the use of *mursal hadiths* from the *tābi'īn*, while the scholars of hadith generally class them as weak. Some major scholars, such as 'Ali ibn al-Madīni and Yaḥyā ibn Sa'īd,=

C. Forbidden Actions by those Present

1) Wailing

The Prophet (ﷺ) strictly forbade wailing and screaming, or the hiring of mourners. Furthermore, he identified such practices as acts of *kufr* (disbelief), because they indicate displeasure with what Allah has decreed. *Eemān* (faith) includes the belief that Allah is the source of all good and that all of His actions are wise. Proper *eemān* would never allow those who possess it to commit such acts of ignorance.

عَنْ أَبِي هُرَيْرَةَ قَالَ: قَالَ رَسُولُ اللَّهِ ﷺ : ((اثْنَتَانِ فِي النَّاسِ هُمَا بِهِمْ كُفْرٌ: الطَّعْنُ فِي النَّسَبِ وَالنِّيَاحَةُ عَلَى الْمَيِّتِ)).

Abu Hurayrah narrated that the Prophet (Blessings and Peace be upon him) said,

> *"There are two practices found among people, both of which indicate disbelief:*[44] *ridiculing the ancestry (of others) and wailing over the dead."*[45]

=differentiated between *mursal hadiths* of *tābi'īn* such as az-Zuhri, who would report from weak narrators, and *tābi'īn* such as Sa'īd ibn Musayyib, whose *mursal hadiths* were all from the *sahābah*, 'Ali ibn al-Madīni accepted Mujāhid's *mursal hadiths*. See *Jāmi' at-Taḥṣīl fi Aḥkām al-Marāsīl*, p. 37.

[44] An-Nawawi mentioned a variety of possible explanations for this statement: 1) these are actions of disbelief and morals of pre-Islamic Ignorance; 2) such actions can lead a person to become a disbeliever; 3) the *kufr* referred to here is the linguistic meaning, i.e., ingratitude; 4) a person who considers such behaviour to be lawful is a disbeliever. *Sharḥ an-Nawawi 'alā Ṣaḥīḥ Muslim*, vol. 1, p. 334.

[45] Muslim (English trans), vol. 1, p. 44, hadith no. 128.

'Abdullah ibn 'Umar also related that Ḥafṣah[46] cried when 'Umar died and he said to her, "Take it easy." Don't you know that the Messenger of Allah (ﷺ) said,

((إِنَّ الْمَيِّتَ يُعَذَّبُ بِبُكَاءِ أَهْلِهِ عَلَيْهِ)).

> *"Verily the dead are punished in their graves by the wailing of their family members over them."*[47]

The dead will suffer due to the wailing of relatives in two cases:

a) When the deceased requested wailing prior to his death.

b) If the deceased knew that was wailing from the customs of his people, yet he did not request that they refrain from it.

2) Striking Cheeks and Tearing Clothes

It was the practice in Arabia at the time of the Prophet (ﷺ) for women in mourning to slap or scratch their cheeks and to rip their clothes. These acts were strictly forbidden, as well as all similar practices which involved self punishment and the destruction of material wealth. These practices all aim at heightening the pain and sorrow accompanying death while Islam seeks to minimize it. Ibn Mas'ūd reported that the Prophet (Blessings and Peace be upon him) said,

((لَيْسَ مِنَّا مَنْ ضَرَبَ الْخُدُودَ وَشَقَّ الْجُيُوبَ وَدَعَا بِدَعْوَى الْجَاهِلِيَّةِ)).

---

[46] Ḥafṣah was one of the Prophet's wives and daughter of 'Umar ibn al-Khaṭṭāb, the second caliph.

[47] Bukhari (Arabic-English), vol. 2, p. 213, hadith no. 379, Muslim (English trans), vol. 2, p. 439, hadith no. 2015, *Sunan Abi Dāwūd*, vol. 2, p. 891, hadith no. 3123, *Sunan Ibn Mājah*,

"Whoever slaps his face, tears his clothes or invites (others) to an un-Islamic slogan is not of us."[48]

3) Shaving the Head or Disheveling[49] the Hair

It was the custom among Arabs prior to Islam that women in mourning shunned all forms of beautification. They used to either shave all of their hair or dishevel it and leave it in a state of disarray, since the women's hair is considered part of her beauty.

In Islam women are required to shun various forms of beautification in order to avoid attracting other men during their period of mourning, since contracting marriage during that period is forbidden. However, shaving the head and disheveling the hair are prohibited, as these acts go beyond normal bounds and are associated with pre-Islamic concepts.

أَبُو بُرْدَةَ بْنُ أَبِي مُوسَى قَالَ: وَجِعَ أَبُو مُوسَى وَجَعًا شَدِيدًا فَغُشِيَ عَلَيْهِ وَرَأْسُهُ فِي حَجْرِ امْرَأَةٍ مِنْ أَهْلِهِ، فَصَاحَتِ امْرَأَة مِن أَهلِهِ فَلَمْ يَسْتَطِعْ أَنْ يَرُدَّ عَلَيْهَا شَيْئًا، فَلَمَّا أَفَاقَ قَالَ: أَنَا بَرِيءٌ مِمَّنْ بَرِئَ مِنْهُ رَسُولُ اللَّهِ ﷺ ، فَإِنَّ رَسُولَ اللَّهِ ﷺ بَرِئَ مِنَ الصَّالِقَةِ وَالْحَالِقَةِ وَالشَّاقَّةِ.

Abu Burdah ibn Abi Mūsā related that Abu Mūsā was overcome by severe pain and lost consciousness while his head was in the lap of one of the women of his family. The woman began to scream, but he was unable to say anything to her. When he

---

[48] Collected by Bukhari, Muslim, Ibn Mājah and al-Bayhaqi; Bukhari (Arabic-English), vol. 2, p. 216, hadith no. 385, Muslim (English trans), vol. 1, p. 59, hadith no. 184, *Sunan Ibn Mājah*, vol. 2, p. 438, hadith no. 1584, and *Mishkāt al-Maṣābīḥ*, vol. 1, p. 361.

[49] i.e. messing it up and leaving it that way.

regained consciousness, he said, "I am blameless of what Allah's Messenger (ﷺ) declared himself blameless: the wailing woman, the one who shaves her head, and the one who tears her clothes."[50]

عن أَسِيدُ بْنُ أَبِي أَسِيدٍ عَنِ امْرَأَةٍ مِنَ الْمُبَايِعَاتِ قَالَتْ: كَانَ فِيمَا أَخَذَ عَلَيْنَا رَسُولُ اللَّهِ ﷺ فِي الْمَعْرُوفِ الَّذِي أَخَذَ عَلَيْنَا أَنْ لاَ نَعْصِيَهُ فِيهِ أَنْ لاَ نَخْمُشَ وَجْهًا وَلاَ نَدْعُوَ وَيْلاً وَلاَ نَشُقَّ جَيْبًا وَأَنْ لاَ نَنْشُرَ شَعَرًا.

Asīd ibn Abi Asīd[51] stated that one of the women who made the pledge to the Prophet (ﷺ) before the Hijrah[52] said, "Among the things which the Prophet (ﷺ) made us pledge obedience to him, was that we should not scratch or slap our faces nor call out "woe", nor rip our clothes nor dishevel our hair."[53]

Those men who normally shave their faces, (which is Islamically incorrect,) but let their beards grow for a few days to indicate their sorrow, fall under this category of disheveling hair, as the intent is similar. This practice is also *bid'ah*, an innovation in the rites of Islam, and is thus forbidden.

---

[50] Bukhari (Arabic-English), vol. 2, p. 215, hadith no. 383, Muslim (English trans), vol. 1, p. 59, hadith nos. 186-7, *Sunan Abi Dāwūd* vol. 2, Pp. 891-92, hadith no. 3124, *Sunan Ibn Mājah*, vol. 2, p. 439, hadith no. 1586, and *Mishkāt al-Maṣābīḥ*, vol. 1, p. 361.

[51] In the English translation, the narrator's name is given incorrectly as Usayd ibn Abu Usayd. See *Taqrīb at-Tahdhīb*, p. 111, hadith no. 510.

[52] The Prophet's migration to the city of Madīnah.

[53] *Sunan Abi Dāwūd*, vol. 2, p. 892, hadith no. 3125, and *Sunan Ibn Mājah*, vol. 2, p. 435, hadith no. 1579, and authenticated by Shaykh al-Albāni in *Ṣaḥīḥ Sunan Abi Dāwūd*, vol. 2, p. 605, hadith no. 2685.

4) Announcing Someone's Death

It is forbidden in Islam to make a big affair about announcing anyone's death, such as proclaiming it from the minarets of the mosques, announcing it in the market streets, etc.;

كَانَ حُذَيْفَةُ إِذَا مَاتَ لَهُ الْمَيِّتُ قَالَ: لاَ تُؤْذِنُوا بِهِ أَحَدًا. إِنِّي أَخَافُ أَنْ يَكُونَ نَعْيًا. إِنِّي سَمِعْتُ رَسُولَ اللَّهِ ﷺ بِأُذُنَيَّ هَاتَيْنِ يَنْهَى عَنِ النَّعْيِ.

If someone died, Hudhayfah ibn al-Yamān used to say, "Do not proclaim his death to anyone, for I fear that it may be a death announcement and I heard Allah's Messenger (ﷺ) forbid the death announcement with my own two ears."[54]

However, a calmly expressed general announcement is allowed, based on the Prophet's practice.

عَنْ أَبِي هُرَيْرَةَ رضي الله عنه قَالَ: نَعَى النَّبِي ﷺ إِلَى أَصْحَابِهِ النَّجَاشِي ثُمَّ تَقَدَّمَ فَصَفُّوا خَلْفَهُ فَكَبَّرَ أَرْبَعًا.

Abu Hurayrah narrated that on the very day that the Najāshi died, Allah's Messenger (ﷺ) announced his death to his Companions, then he stepped forward and they lined up behind him and he made (a funeral prayer consisting of) four *takbīrs*.[55]

5) Gathering to Give Condolences

The custom of organizing gatherings in the home, at the grave or in the masjid to give condolences to the family of the deceased is

---

[54] Collected by Tirmidhi and in *Sunan Ibn Mājah*, vol. 2, p. 382, hadith no. 1476, and authenticated by Shaykh al-Albāni in *Ṣaḥīḥ Sunan Ibn Mājah*, vol. 1, p. 248, hadith no. 1203.

[55] Bukhari (Arabic-English), vol. 2, p. 227, hadith no. 404, Muslim (English trans), vol. 2, p. 452, hadith no. 2077 & 2078, *Sunan Abi Dāwūd*, vol. 2, p. 911, hadith no. 3198, and *Mishkāt al-Maṣābīḥ*, vol. 1, p. 348.

against the Sunnah of the Companions of the Prophet.

عَنْ جَرِيرِ بْنِ عَبْدِ اللَّهِ الْبَجَلِيِّ قَالَ: كُنَّا نَرَى الاِجْتِمَاعَ إِلَى أَهْلِ الْمَيِّتِ وَصَنْعَةَ الطَّعَامِ مِنَ النِّيَاحَةِ.

Jarīr ibn ‘Abdillah al-Bajali was quoted as saying, “We used to regard gathering at the home of the deceased’s family and their preparation of food an aspect of wailing.”[56]

Imām ash-Shāfi‘i said, “I dislike gatherings, even if there is no wailing or crying. For it only renews the (family’s feelings of) sorrow and puts burdens on their food supplies.”[57] Imām an-Nawawi related that the leading scholars prohibited organized gatherings, based on its being an innovation.[58]

6) Preparing Food by the Family of the Deceased

The obligation placed on the family of the dead person to prepare food for gatherings is incorrect, based on the previously mentioned statement of the Prophets Companion, al-Bajali. Furthermore, it contradicts the Prophet’s explicit instruction to relatives, friends and neighbours to send food to the bereaved family.

عَنْ عَبْدِ اللَّهِ ابْنِ جَعْفَرٍ قَالَ: لَمَّا جَاءَ نَعْيُ جَعْفَرٍ قَالَ النَّبِيُّ ﷺ : ((اصْنَعُوا لِأَهْلِ جَعْفَرٍ طَعَامًا، فَقَدْ أَتَاهُمْ مَا يَشْغَلُهُمْ)).

‘Abdullah ibn Ja‘far related that when the announcement of Ja‘far’s death came, the Messenger of Allah (ﷺ) said,

---

[56] *Sunan Ibn Mājah*, vol. 2, p. 456, hadith no. 1612, and authenticated by Shaykh al-Albāni in *Ṣaḥīḥ Sunan Ibn Mājah*, vol. 1, p. 269, hadith no. 1308.

[57] Al-Umm, vol. 1, p. 248, quoted in *Aḥkām al-Janā’iz*, p. 167.

[58] *Al-Majmū‘*, vol. 5, p. 306, quoted in *Aḥkām al-Janā’iz*, p. 167.

> *"Prepare food for Ja'far's family, for something has happened to them which is distracting them (from their needs)."*[59]

عَنْ عُرْوَةَ عَنْ عَائِشَةَ رَضِي اللَّهُ عَنْهَا أَنَّهَا كَانَتْ تَأْمُرُ بِالتَّلْبِينِ لِلمَرِيضِ وَلِلْمَحْزُونِ عَلَى الهَالِكِ وَكَانَتْ تَقُولُ: إِنِّي سَمِعْتُ رَسُولَ اللَّهِ ﷺ يَقُولُ: ((إِنَّ التَّلْبِينَةَ تُجِمُّ فُؤَادَ الْمَرِيضِ وَتَذْهَبُ بِبَعْضِ الْحُزْنِ)).

'Urwah stated that 'Ā'ishah used to recommend *talbīnah*[60] for the sick and those grieving over a death. She used to say, "I heard Allah's Messenger (ﷺ) say,

> *"Indeed, talbīnah relaxes the heart of the sick and removes some of their sorrow."*[61]

D. Recommended Actions by Those Present

1) Preparing food for the family of the deceased

It was the practice of the Prophet (ﷺ) to have his family prepare food for the relatives of the dead.

عَنْ أَسْمَاءَ بِنْتِ عُمَيْسٍ قَالَتْ: لَمَّا أُصِيبَ جَعْفَرٌ رَجَعَ رَسُولُ اللَّهِ ﷺ إِلَى أَهْلِهِ فَقَالَ: ((إِنَّ آلَ جَعْفَرٍ قَدْ شُغِلُوا بِشَأْنِ مَيِّتِهِمْ فَاصْنَعُوا لَهُمْ طَعَامًا)). قَالَ عَبْدُ اللَّهِ: فَمَا زَالَتْ سُنَّةً حَتَّى كَانَ حَدِيثًا فَتُرِكَ.

---

[59] Collected by Tirmidhi, Abu Dāwūd and Ibn Mājah (*Sunan Ibn Mājah*, vol. 2, p. 455, hadith no. 1610) and authenticated by Shaykh al-Albāni in *Ṣaḥīḥ Sunan ibn Mājah*, vol. 1, p. 268, hadith no. 1306.

[60] Porridge made from flour, bran and honey.

[61] Bukhari (Arabic-English), vol. 7, p. 401, hadith no. 593, and Muslim (English trans), vol. 4, p. 1202, hadith no. 5491.

Asmā' bint 'Umays said, "When Ja'far was killed, Allah's Messenger (ﷺ) returned to his family and said, "*Ja'far's family is distracted by the affairs of their dead, so prepare some food for them.*" 'Abdullah[62] said, "That remained the Sunnah until it became an innovation[63] and was abandoned.[64]"

2) Praising the dead

It is recommended that righteous Muslims who knew the deceased well and were among his or her neighbours should testify to others about the good qualities of the deceased. This is a means of reminding others of righteousness and spurring them on to do good deeds. The Prophet (ﷺ) personally encouraged this practice and pointed out that such praise is of benefit to the dead person.

عَنْ أَبِي الْأَسْوَدِ قَالَ: قَدِمْتُ الْمَدِينَةَ وَقَدْ وَقَعَ بِهَا مَرَضٌ فَجَلَسْتُ إِلَى عُمَرَ بْنِ الْخَطَّابِ رضي الله عنه فَمَرَّتْ بِهِمْ جَنَازَةٌ فَأُثْنِيَ عَلَى صَاحِبِهَا خَيْرًا فَقَالَ عُمَرُ رضي الله عنه: وَجَبَتْ. ثُمَّ مُرَّ بِأُخْرَى فَأُثْنِيَ عَلَى صَاحِبِهَا خَيْرًا فَقَالَ عُمَرُ رضي الله عنه: وَجَبَتْ. ثُمَّ مُرَّ بِالثَّالِثَةِ فَأُثْنِيَ عَلَى صَاحِبِهَا شَرًّا فَقَالَ: وَجَبَتْ. فَقَالَ أَبُو الْأَسْوَدِ: فَقُلْتُ: وَمَا وَجَبَتْ يَا أَمِيرَ الْمُؤْمِنِينَ؟ قَالَ: قُلْتُ كَمَا قَالَ النَّبِيُّ ﷺ: ((أَيُّمَا مُسْلِمٍ شَهِدَ لَهُ أَرْبَعَةٌ بِخَيْرٍ أَدْخَلَهُ اللَّهُ الْجَنَّةَ)).

Abul-Aswad narrated that he came to Madīnah during the time of an epidemic and he sat next to 'Umar ibn al-Khaṭṭāb. When a bier

---

[62] 'Abdullah ibn Abi Bakr was one of the later narrators of this hadith.

[63] People later elaborated on this practice until it became an exaggerated ritual with much pomp and show. Later scholars considered its distorted form an innovation and abandoned it.

[64] *Sunan Ibn Mājah*, vol. 2, p. 455, hadith no. 1610, and authenticated by Shaykh al-Albāni in *Ṣaḥīḥ Sunan Ibn Mājah*, vol. 1, Pp. 268-9, hadith no. 1307.

passed by, the people praised the person and 'Umar said, "It has been affirmed." Another bier passed by and the people praised the person and again 'Umar said, "It has been affirmed." When a third bier passed by, the people spoke badly of the deceased then 'Umar said, "It has been affirmed." Abul-Aswad asked him what was affirmed and he replied, "I said what the Prophet (ﷺ) said,

> *"Allah will put in Paradise any Muslim for whom four have testified to his goodness."*[65]

عَنْ أَنَسٍ أَنَّ النَّبِيَّ ﷺ قَالَ: ((مَا مِنْ مُسْلِمٍ يَمُوتُ فَيَشْهَدُ لَهُ أَرْبَعَةٌ أَهْلُ أَبْيَاتٍ مِنْ جِيرَانِهِ الأَدْنَيْنَ إِلاَّ قَالَ: قَدْ قَبِلْتُ فِيهِ عِلْمَكُمْ فِيهِ وَغَفَرْتُ لَهُ مَا لاَ تَعْلَمُونَ)).

Anas quoted the Prophet (ﷺ) as saying,

> *"For any Muslim who dies and four of his close neighbours testify that they have known him to be good, Allah; the Blessed, the Highest, will say, "I have accepted your testimony and forgiven him for what you do not know about.""*[66]

The practice of requesting witnesses after the burial prayer and the bearing of witness by those who do not even know the deceased is *bid'ah* and futile, for false testimony will never benefit anyone in the next life.

---

[65] Bukhari (Arabic-English), vol. 2, Pp. 253-54, hadith no. 449, *Mishkāt al-Maṣābīḥ*, vol. 1, p. 350.

[66] Collected by Aḥmad and authenticated in *Aḥkām al-Janā'iz*, Pp. 45-6.

passed by [illegible] It has been affirmed. [illegible] the [illegible] bier passed by [illegible] people spoke [illegible] said, "It has been affirmed." [illegible] was affirmed and [illegible] replied, "[illegible]

"[illegible]"

[illegible]

Anas quoted the Prophet (ﷺ) as saying:

"[illegible] Muslim [illegible] neighbours testify that they [illegible] Allah [illegible] accepted [illegible] testimony and forgive [illegible]"

The practice of [illegible] witnesses after the burial prayer and the bearing of [illegible] those who do not even know the deceased is *bid'ah* and [illegible] false testimony will not benefit anyone in the next life.

[illegible] Bukhari (Arabic-English), vol. 2, pp. 253-4 [illegible] *Muslim*, vol. 1, [illegible]

[illegible] Collected by [illegible] authenticated in *Ahkam* [illegible] pp. 45-6.

CHAPTER 3: PREPARING THE BODY

There should be no delay in the washing, shrouding and burial of the deceased, as was mentioned earlier and supported by the Prophet's instruction, "*Hasten the funeral rites*."[1]

A. Injunctions Concerning Washing

1 *Farḍ Kifāyah* (Collective Obligation)

Washing the dead body prior to shrouding and burial is obligatory, according to numerous recorded instructions given by the Prophet (ﷺ). For example, when his daughter, Zaynab, passed away, he (ﷺ) told the women who were preparing her for burial,

((اغْسِلْنَهَا))

"*You should wash her...*"[2]

This obligation is however considered *Farḍ Kifāyah* (a collective responsibility), if there is no one to claim the body. If someone

---

[1] Collected in all of the six books of hadith. Bukhari (Arabic-English), vol. 2, p. 225, hadith no. 401, Muslim (English trans), vol. 2, p. 448, hadith no. 2059, *Sunan Abi Dāwūd*, vol. 2, Pp. 897-8, hadith no. 3153, *Sunan Ibn Mājah*, vol. 2, p. 382, hadith no. 1477 and *Mishkāt al-Maṣābīḥ*, vol. 1, p. 338.

[2] Reported by Umm 'Aṭīyah and collected in all the six books of hadith. Bukhari (Arabic-English), vol. 2, p. 194, hadith no. 344, Muslim (English trans), vol. 2, p. 445, hadith no. 2041, *Sunan Abi Dāwūd* vol. 2, p. 894, hadith no. 3136, *Sunan Ibn Mājah*, vol. 2, p. 372, hadith no. 1458, *Muwaṭṭa*, p. 105, hadith no. 514 and *Mishkāt al-Maṣābīḥ*, vol. 1, p. 344.

performs the washing, the community is freed from the obligation, but if no one does it, the whole community shares in the sin of not having fulfilled the obligation.

2) Males Wash Males

As a general rule, males should take the responsibility of washing males, and females should wash females. This rule is to avoid the arousal of any undesirable feelings during this delicate procedure. The only exception to the rule is in the case of husband and wife, or small children. Permission for husbands to wash their wives and vice versa is based primarily on the fact that there is no prohibition from doing so. It is also based on statements of the Prophet (ﷺ) and his wives.

عَنْ عَائِشَةَ قَالَتْ رَجَعَ رَسُولُ اللَّهِ ﷺ مِنَ الْبَقِيعِ فَوَجَدَنِي وَأَنَا أَجِدُ صُدَاعًا فِي رَأْسِي وَأَنَا أَقُولُ وَا رَأْسَاهُ فَقَالَ: ((بَلْ أَنَا يَا عَائِشَةُ وَا رَأْسَاهُ)) ثُمَّ قَالَ: ((مَا ضَرَّكِ لَوْ مِتِّ قَبْلِي فَقُمْتُ عَلَيْكِ فَغَسَّلْتُكِ وَكَفَّنْتُكِ وَصَلَّيْتُ عَلَيْكِ وَدَفَنْتُكِ)).

'Ā'ishah reported that when the Prophet (ﷺ) returned from a funeral at al-Baqi', she was suffering from a headache and said, "Oh my head." The Prophet (ﷺ) replied, *"No, it is I who am in pain from whatever hurts you. If you were to die before me, I would wash you, shroud you, pray for you and bury you."*[3]

عَنْ عَائِشَةَ قَالَتْ: لَوْ كُنْتُ اسْتَقْبَلْتُ مِنْ أَمْرِي مَا اسْتَدْبَرْتُ مَا غَسَلَ النَّبِيَّ ﷺ غَيْرُ نِسَائِهِ.

---

[3] Collected by Ibn Mājah (*Sunan Ibn Mājah*, vol. 2, p. 376, hadith no. 1465), Aḥmad and ad-Dārimi and authenticated by Shaykh al-Albāni in *Ṣaḥīḥ Sunan Ibn Mājah*, vol. 1, p. 247, hadith no. 1197. See also *Mishkāt al-Maṣābīḥ*, Vol. 2, p. 1308.

'Ā'ishah said, "If I had known beforehand what I came to know afterwards, only the wives of the Prophet (ﷺ) would have washed him."[4]

3) The Most Knowledgeable

The most knowledgeable people about the procedures should be responsible for washing the dead body, preferably from among the deceased's immediate family members or relatives. Such was the case of those who took charge of washing the Prophet (ﷺ). They were his cousins, 'Ali ibn Abi Ṭālib, and al-Faḍl ibn 'Abbās, and Usāmah, the son of the Prophet's adopted son, Zayd ibn Ḥārithah.[5]

عَنْ عَلِيِّ بْنِ أَبِي طَالِبٍ قَالَ لَمَّا غَسَّلَ النَّبِيَّ ﷺ ذَهَبَ يَلْتَمِسُ مِنْهُ مَا يَلْتَمِسُ مِنَ الْمَيِّتِ فَلَمْ يَجِدْهُ فَقَالَ: بِأَبِي الطَّيِّبُ طِبْتَ حَيًّا وَطِبْتَ مَيِّتًا.

'Ali ibn Abi Ṭālib is reported to have said that when he bathed the Prophet (ﷺ), he began to search for traces of impurities which are usually found on dead bodies, but he did not find any. So he said, "May my father be a ransom for you. You are the most pure. You were clean and pure in life and you are clean and pure after your demise."[6]

---

[4] *Sunan Ibn Mājah*, vol. 2, p. 376, hadith no. 1464 and *Sunan Abi Dāwūd*, vol. 2, p. 894, hadith no. 3135 and authenticated by Shaykh al-Albāni in *Ṣaḥīḥ Sunan Ibn Mājah*, vol. 1, p. 247, hadith no. 1196. 'Ā'ishah's reference to what she came to know afterwards seems to be about the *fitnah* that developed out of the fact that 'Ali washed the Prophet's body. This led to some people accusing the other leading *ṣaḥābah* of being concerned only with grabbing for power while 'Ali washed the body.

[5] *Sunan Abi Dāwūd*, vol. 2, p. 912, hadith no. 3203 and authenticated by Shaykh al-Albāni in *Ṣaḥīḥ Sunan Abi Dāwūd*, vol. 2, p. 618, hadith no. 2748.

[6] *Sunan Ibn Mājah*, vol. 2, p. 377, hadith no. 1467 and authenticated by Shaykh al-Albāni in *Ṣaḥīḥ Sunan Ibn Mājah*, vol. 1, p. 247, hadith no. 1198.

If relatives are unavailable, it is recommended that pious individuals wash the body, due to the delicate nature of this procedure. Those who deal with the dead in hospitals and morgues, usually become quite callous, rough or disrespectful in their treatment of the corpses. The same is true of those hired to wash the dead. Consequently, God-fearing individuals should be chosen in order to ensure proper treatment of the dead.

4 *Ghusl* (Islamic Bath)

Those who wash the dead are not required to be in a state of purity. Consequently, menstruating women may perform the washing procedure. However, it is recommended that those who wash the dead take an Islamic bath (*ghusl*) afterwards, based on the following hadiths:

عَنْ أَبِي هُرَيْرَةَ قَالَ: قَالَ رَسُولُ اللَّهِ ﷺ: ((مَنْ غَسَّلَ مَيِّتًا فَلْيَغْتَسِلْ وَمَنْ حَمَلَهُ فَلْيَتَوَضَأْ)).

Abu Hurayrah reported that the Prophet (ﷺ) said,

> *"Whoever washes the dead should take a ghusl and whoever carries the corpse should make wuḍū."*[7]

The order in the above-mentioned hadith is understood as a recommendation due to the following hadith in which Ibn 'Abbās quoted the Prophet (ﷺ) as saying,

((لَيْسَ عَلَيْكُمْ فِي غُسْلِ مَيِّتِكُمْ غُسْلٌ إِذَا غَسَلْتُمُوهُ، فَإِنَّ مَيِّتَكُمْ لَيْسَ بِنَجِسٍ، فَحَسْبُكُمْ أَنْ تَغْسِلُوا أَيْدِيَكُمْ))

---

[7] *Sunan Abi Dāwūd*, vol.2, p. 898, hadith no. 3155, *Sunan Ibn Mājah*, vol. 2, Pp. 374-5, hadith no. 1463 and *Mishkāt al-Maṣābīḥ*, vol. 1, p. 108, and authenticated by Shaykh al-Albāni in *Ṣaḥīḥ Sunan Abi Dāwūd*, vol. 2, p. 609, hadith no. 2707.

> *"You are not required to make ghusl if you have washed your dead, for verily your dead are not impure.*[8] *It is sufficient for you to wash your hands."*[9]

Ibn 'Umar is also reported to have said, "Whenever we used to wash the dead, some of us used to make *ghusl*, while others would not."[10]

5) Method of washing

First: The body should be laid out, stripped of its garments and its joints loosened, if possible. A cloth should be placed over the private parts, between the navel and the knee, and the stomach should be pressed to expel any remaining impurities.

عَنْ عَائِشَةَ رَضِيَ اللَّهُ عَنْهَا قَالَتْ : لَمَّا أَرادُوا غَسْلَ النَّبِي قَالُوا: وَاللَّهِ مَانَدْرِي، أَنُجَرِّدُ رَسُولَ اللَّهِ مِنْ ثِيَابِهِ كَمَا نُجَرِّدُ مَوْتَانَا، أَمْ نُغَسِّلُهُ وَعَلَيْهِ ثِيَابُهُ؟

'Ā'ishah said, "When they wanted to wash the Prophet (ﷺ), they said, "By Allah, we don't know whether we should remove all of Allah's Messenger's clothes as we undress our dead, or whether we should wash him with his clothes on?"[11]

Second: A rag or cloth should be used to wash the body beginning with the places on the right side of the body washed during *wuḍū*.

---

[8] The Arabic *najis* means ritually impure according to Islam.

[9] Collected by al-Bayhaqi and al-Ḥākim and authenticated in *Aḥkām al-Janā'iz*, p. 54.

[10] Collected by al-Dāraquṭni and authenticated in *Aḥkām al-Janā'iz*, Pp. 53-54.

[11] *Sunan Abi Dāwūd*, vol. 2, p. 894, hadith no. 3135 and authenticated in *Aḥkām al-Janā'iz*, p. 49.

عَنْ أُمِّ عَطِيَّةَ رَضِي اللَّهُ عَنْهَا قَالَتْ دَخَلَ عَلَيْنَا رَسُولُ اللَّهِ ﷺ وَنَحْنُ نَغْسِلُ ابْنَتَهُ فَقَالَ : ((ابْدَءُوا بِمَيَامِنِهَا وَمَوَاضِعِ الْوُضُوءِ مِنْهَا)).

Umm 'Aṭīyah said, "The Messenger of Allah (ﷺ) came among us while we were bathing his daughter and said, "*Begin with her right side and the places of wuḍū.*"[12]

Third: After completing the *wuḍū*, the woman's hair should be undone if it had been braided and the hair thoroughly washed. Then the rest of the body should be washed, turning the body on its side so as to complete the right side before washing the left.

عَنْ أُمِّ عَطِيَّةَ رَضِي اللَّهُ عَنْهَا إِنَّهُنَّ جَعَلْنَ رَأْسَ بِنْتِ رَسُولُ اللَّهِ ﷺ ثَلاثَةَ قُرُونٍ، نَقَضْنَهُ ثُمَّ غَسَلْنَهُ ثُمَّ جَعَلْنَهُ ثَلاثَةَ قُرُونٍ.

Umm 'Aṭīyah said that they plaited the hair of the Messenger of Allah's daughter in three braids. They first undid her hair, washed it and then plaited it in three braids.[13]

Fourth: The body should be washed a minimum of three times and the water should have some cleaning agent in it, like soap or disinfectant. The final washing should have some perfume in it, like camphor or the like.

عَنْ أُمِّ عَطِيَّةَ رَضِي اللَّهُ عَنْهَا قَالَتْ دَخَلَ عَلَيْنَا رَسُولُ اللَّهِ ﷺ وَنَحْنُ نَغْسِلُ ابْنَتَهُ فَقَالَ: ((اغْسِلْنَهَا ثَلاثًا أَوْ خَمْسًا أَوْ أَكْثَرَ مِنْ ذَلِكَ بِمَاءٍ وَسِدْرٍ وَاجْعَلْنَ فِي الآخِرَةِ كَافُورًا)).

---

[12] Bukhari (Arabic-English), vol. 2, p. 195, hadith no. 346, Muslim (English trans), vol. 2, p. 446, hadith no. 2048, *Sunan Abi Dāwūd*, vol. 2, p. 895, hadith no. 3139, *Sunan Ibn Mājah*, vol. 2, Pp. 372-3, hadith nos. 1459 and *Mishkāt al-Maṣābīḥ*, vol. 1, p. 344.

[13] Bukhari (Arabic-English), vol. 2, p. 197, hadith no. 350.

Umm 'Aṭīyah said, "Allah's Messenger (ﷺ) came among us while we were washing his daughter and said,

> *"Wash her three, or five or more times,*[14] *using lotus water and put camphor in the last washing."*[15]

Fifth: The body should then be dried and the hair combed out. In the case of women, the hair should be plaited into three braids one from the front and two from the sides and placed behind her head. This practice is based on Umm 'Aṭīyah's statement,

((ضَفَرْنَا شَعَرَ بِنْتِ النَّبِيِّ ﷺ تَعْنِي ثَلاَثَةَ قُرُونٍ)) وَقَالَ وَكِيعٌ : قَالَ سُفْيَانُ : نَاصِيَتُهَا وَقَرْنَيْهَا.

"We braided the Prophet's daughter's hair in three braids." Waki' quoted Sufyān as saying, "One (braid) from the forelock and two at the sides.[16]"

Sixth: Exceptions

The Pilgrim: In the case of person who died in the state of *Iḥrām*[17] perfume should not be used in washing his or her body.

---

[14] 'Seven times' and 'an odd number of times' were mentioned in other narrations collected in Bukhari (Arabic-English), vol. 2, Pp. 196-7, hadith no. 349.

[15] Bukhari (Arabic-English), vol. 2, p. 194, hadith no. 344, Muslim (English trans), vol. 2, p. 445, hadith no. 2041, *Sunan Abi Dāwūd*, vol. 2, p. 894, hadith no. 3136, *Sunan Ibn Mājah*, vol. 2, p. 372, hadith nos. 1458 and *Mishkāt al-Maṣābīḥ*, vol. 1, p. 344.

[16] Bukhari (Arabic-English), vol. 2, p. 198, hadith no. 352, Muslim (English trans), vol. 2, p. 446, hadith no. 2047, *Sunan Abi Dāwūd*, vol. 2, p. 895, hadith no. 3138, *Sunan Ibn Mājah*, vol. 2, Pp. 372-3, hadith nos. 1458-9 and *Mishkāt al-Maṣābīḥ*, vol. 1, p. 344.

[17] One who has made the intention for Ḥajj or 'Umrah and donned the prescribed garments.

عَنِ ابْنِ عَبَّاسٍ رَضِيَ اللَّهُ عَنْهُمْ أَنَّ رَجُلاً وَقَصَهُ بَعِيرُهُ وَنَحْنُ مَعَ النَّبِيِّ ﷺ وَهُوَ مُحْرِمٌ فَقَالَ النَّبِيُّ ﷺ : ((اغْسِلُوهُ بِمَاءٍ وَسِدْرٍ وَكَفِّنُوهُ فِي ثَوْبَيْنِ وَلاَ تُمِسُّوهُ طِيبًا وَلاَ تُخَمِّرُوا رَأْسَهُ فَإِنَّ اللَّهَ يَبْعَثُهُ يَوْمَ الْقِيَامَةِ مُلَبِّيًا)).

Ibn 'Abbās reported that while they were with the Prophet (Blessings and Peace be upon him), a man in a state of *iḥrām* was thrown by his camel and he said,

> *"Wash him with water and (ground leaves of the) lote-tree,*[18] *and shroud him in two pieces of cloth. But don't put perfume on him nor cover his head, for Allah will resurrect him on the Day of Judgement calling out the talbīyah."*[19]

The martyr: In the case of the martyr (*shahīd*), his or her body should not be washed at all, but should be buried as it is.

عَنْ جَابِرِ بْنِ عَبْدِ اللَّهِ عَنِ النَّبِيِّ ﷺ أَنَّهُ قَالَ فِي قَتْلَى أُحُدٍ : ((لاَ تُغَسِّلُوهُمْ فَإِنَّ كُلَّ جُرْحٍ أَوْ كُلَّ دَمٍ يَفُوحُ مِسْكًا يَوْمَ الْقِيَامَةِ.)) وَلَمْ يُصَلِّ عَلَيْهِمْ.

Jābir also reported that the Prophet (ﷺ) said regarding those killed during the battle of Uḥud,

> *"Do not wash them for verily every wound will emit musk on the Day of Judgement."* And he did not offer

[18] The Arabic term '*sidr*' refers to the lote-tree of which there are two species; one grows in cultivated lands and its ground leaves are used in bathing (*ghusl*) and its fruit (*nabq*) is sweet; and the other grows in the desert, and its leaves are not used and its fruit is juicy. (*Arabic-English Lexicon*, vol. 1, p. 1331).

[19] Bukhari (Arabic-English), vol. 2, Pp. 200-1, hadith no. 357 and *Sunan Abi Dāwūd* vol. 2, p. 920, hadith no. 3235.

the funeral prayer for them.[20]

B. Injunctions Concerning the Shroud

1) Shrouding the body is obligatory, based on the commands of the Prophet (ﷺ) to do so. The body should be shrouded immediately after it is washed and dried.

عَنِ ابْنِ عَبَّاسٍ رَضِيَ اللَّهُ عَنْهُمَا أَنَّ رَجُلاً وَقَصَهُ بَعِيرُهُ وَنَحْنُ مَعَ النَّبِيِّ ﷺ وَهُوَ مُحْرِمٌ فَقَالَ النَّبِيُّ ﷺ : ((اغْسِلُوهُ بِمَاءٍ وَسِدْرٍ وَكَفِّنُوهُ فِي ثَوْبَيْنِ)).

---

[20] Collected by Aḥmad and authenticated in *Aḥkām al-Janā'iz*, Pp. 54-5, footnote 32. A slightly different version of Jābir's hadith was collected by Bukhari (Arabic-English), vol. 2, p. 239, hadith no. 427 and by Tirmidhi, an-Nasā'i and Ibn Mājah (*Sunan Ibn Mājah*, vol. 2, p. 403, hadith no. 1514). Imām ash-Shāfi'i stated that the reports that the Prophet (ﷺ) didn't pray over the martyrs of Uḥud at the time of their burial is confirmed by numerous reports. (Quoted by Ibn Ḥajar in *Fatḥ al-Bāri*, vol. 3, p. 249.) Ash-Shawkāni and al-Albāni contend that he did pray over them immediately after the battle. There are some hadiths that mention that he did so, while others claim he only prayed over Ḥamzah. The affirmative hadiths collected in the *Sunan* are weak. Al-Albāni quotes two affirmative hadiths reported by aṭ-Ṭabarāni and aṭ-Ṭaḥāwi whose isnāds he ruled to be *ḥasan*. He argues that although the hadith of Jābir is more authentic in its isnad, the information it contains is that an event did not occur, whereas the other hadiths affirm that the event did occur. In such situations, the one who has knowledge of an event is given precedence over one who doesn't. Some scholars say that Jābir was one of those who took their relatives' corpses back to Madīnah to bury them. When the Prophet (ﷺ) found out, he sent a messenger to announce that they should bring back the martyrs and bury them at the battlefield. It was because of this that Jābir missed the Prophet's *ṣalāh* upon the martyrs. The other factor that caused them to favour the affirmative reports is that the basic rules is that *ṣalātu-janāzah* should be performed for dead Muslims. It is interesting to note that nothing authentic is recorded about either *ṣalātul-janāzah* or the lack of it for the martyrs of other battles. See *Nayl al-Awtār*, vol. 4, Pp. 52-6.

Ibn 'Abbās reported that a man in a state of *iḥrām* was thrown by his camel while they were with the Prophet (ﷺ) and he said,

> *"Wash him with water and (ground leaves of the) lote-tree, and shroud him in two pieces of cloth."*[21]

2) The shroud or its cost should be taken from the wealth left behind by the deceased, if there is enough money to purchase garments which can cover all the body.

عَنْ خَبَّابٍ رَضِي اللَّهُ عَنْهُ قَالَ: قُتِلَ يَوْمَ أُحُدٍ فَلَمْ نَجِدْ مَا نُكَفِّنُهُ إِلاَّ بُرْدَةً.

Khabbāb said, "(Muṣ'ab ibn 'Umayr) was killed during the Battle of Uḥud and we couldn't find anything to shroud him in except his cloak."[22]

3) The shroud should be sufficient to cover the whole body. If not, those preparing the body should supply a proper shroud.

عَنْ جَابِرِ بْنِ عَبْدِ اللَّهِ أَنَّ النَّبِيَّ ﷺ خَطَبَ يَوْمًا فَذَكَرَ رَجُلاً مِنْ أَصْحَابِهِ قُبِضَ فَكُفِّنَ فِي كَفَنٍ غَيْرِ طَائِلٍ وَقُبِرَ لَيْلا فَزَجَرَ النَّبِيُّ ﷺ أَنْ يُقْبَرَ الرَّجُلُ بِاللَّيْلِ حَتَّى يُصَلَّى عَلَيْهِ إِلاَّ أَنْ يُضْطَرَّ إِنْسَانٌ إِلَى ذَلِكَ وَقَالَ النَّبِيُّ ﷺ ((إِذَا كَفَّنَ أَحَدُكُمْ أَخَاهُ فَلْيُحَسِّنْ كَفَنَهُ.))

Jābir narrated that one day the Prophet (ﷺ) gave a sermon in which he talked about one of his Companions who had died and had been shrouded in a short shroud and buried at night. He warned against burying (a person) at night, before the funeral

---

[21] Bukhari (Arabic-English), vol. 2, Pp. 200-1, hadith no. 357 and *Sunan Abi Dāwūd* vol. 2, p. 920, hadith no. 3235.

[22] Bukhari (Arabic-English), vol. 2, p. 205, hadith no. 366, Muslim (English trans), vol. 2, Pp. 446-47, hadith no. 2050, *Sunan Abi Dāwūd*, vol. 2, Pp. 896-97, hadith no. 3149 and *Mishkāt al-Maṣābīḥ*, vol. 2, Pp. 1364-65.

prayer could be made for him, unless one was forced to do that. The Prophet (ﷺ) then said,

> *"If any of you shrouds his dead brother (Muslim), he should shroud him well."*[23]

If the shroud is not large enough to cover the whole body and no substitute is available, the head and body should be covered by the shroud and the feet can be covered with twigs.

عَنْ خَبَّابٍ رَضِيَ اللَّهُ عَنْهُ قَالَ: هَاجَرْنَا مَعَ النَّبِيِّ ﷺ نَلْتَمِسُ وَجْهَ اللَّهِ فَوَقَعَ أَجْرُنَا عَلَى اللَّهِ فَمِنَّا مَنْ مَاتَ لَمْ يَأْكُلْ مِنْ أَجْرِهِ شَيْئًا مِنْهُمْ مُصْعَبُ بْنُ عُمَيْرٍ وَمِنَّا مَنْ أَيْنَعَتْ لَهُ ثَمَرَتُهُ فَهُوَ يَهْدِبُهَا قُتِلَ يَوْمَ أُحُدٍ فَلَمْ نَجِدْ مَا نُكَفِّنُهُ إِلاَّ بُرْدَةً إِذَا غَطَّيْنَا بِهَا رَأْسَهُ خَرَجَتْ رِجْلاَهُ وَإِذَا غَطَّيْنَا رِجْلَيْهِ خَرَجَ رَأْسُهُ فَأَمَرَنَا النَّبِيُّ ﷺ أَنْ نُغَطِّيَ رَأْسَهُ وَأَنْ نَجْعَلَ عَلَى رِجْلَيْهِ مِنَ الإِذْخِرِ.

Khabbāb said, "We migrated along with the Prophet (ﷺ) for the sake of Allah so our reward was ensured by Allah. Some of us died without accumulating any material possessions, like Muṣ'ab ibn 'Umayr, while others gained rewards. Muṣ'ab ibn 'Umayr died during the Battle of Uḥud and we couldn't find anything to shroud him in besides his cloak. When we covered his head, his feet were exposed, and when we covered his feet, his head was exposed. So the Prophet (ﷺ) instructed us to cover his head (with his cloak) and cover his feet with twigs."[24]

---

[23] Muslim (English trans), vol. 2, p. 448, hadith no. 2058, *Sunan Abi Dāwūd*, vol. 2, p. 895, hadith no. 3142, *Sunan Ibn Mājah*,vol. 2, p. 380, hadith no. 1474 and *Mishkāt al-Maṣābīḥ*, vol. 1, p. 344.

[24] Bukhari (Arabic-English), vol. 2, p. 205, hadith no. 366, Muslim (English trans), vol. 2, Pp. 446-47, hadith no. 2050, *Sunan Abi Dāwūd*, vol. 2, Pp. 896-97, hadith no. 3149 and *Mishkāt al-Maṣābīḥ*, vol. 2, Pp. 1364-65. The Arabic=

4) If the number of dead is great or the cloth used for shrouding is insufficient for all of the bodies, more than one body may be wrapped in the same shroud at a time.[25]

عَنْ أَنَسِ بْنِ مَالِكٍ ـ الْمَعْنَى ـ أَنَّ رَسُولَ اللَّهِ ﷺ مَرَّ عَلَى حَمْزَةَ وَقَدْ مُثِّلَ بِهِ فَقَالَ لَوْلاَ أَنْ تَجِدَ صَفِيَّةُ فِي نَفْسِهَا لَتَرَكْتُهُ حَتَّى تَأْكُلَهُ الْعَافِيَةُ حَتَّى يُحْشَرَ مِنْ بُطُونِهَا وَقَلَّتِ الثِّيَابُ وَكَثُرَتِ الْقَتْلَى فَكَانَ الرَّجُلُ وَالرَّجُلاَنِ وَالثَّلاَثَةُ يُكَفَّنُونَ فِي الثَّوْبِ الْوَاحِدِ زَادَ قُتَيْبَةُ ثُمَّ يُدْفَنُونَ فِي قَبْرٍ وَاحِدٍ فَكَانَ رَسُولُ اللَّهِ ﷺ يَسْأَلُ أَيُّهُمْ أَكْثَرُ قُرْآنًا فَيُقَدِّمُهُ إِلَى الْقِبْلَةِ.

Anas ibn Mālik related that Allah's Messenger (ﷺ) passed by the mutilated body of Ḥamzah[26] and said, "*Were it not that Ṣafiyah*[27] *would have grieved, I would have left him until the birds and wild animals devoured him so he would be resurrected in their bellies.*" The garments were scanty and the slain were in great in number. <u>So one, two and three persons were shrouded in one sheet</u>

=word translated as "twigs" is *Ithkhir*, a sweet smelling plant which becomes white when dried; used for roofing houses over the wood (*Arabic-English Lexicon*, vol. 1, Pp. 956-7).

[25] See the following narrations: Bukhari (Arabic-English), vol. 2, p. 239, hadith no. 427, *Sunan Abi Dāwūd*, vol. 2, p. 893, hadith no. 3130 and *Sunan Ibn Mājah*, vol. 2, p. 403, hadith no. 1514.

[26] Ḥamzah ibn 'Abdil-Muṭṭalib was the brother of Abu Ṭālib, and an uncle of the Prophet (ﷺ). He was known for his bravery, thus his acceptance of Islam in Makkah greatly strengthened the position of Muslims there. He was killed during the Battle of Uḥud, and Hind bint 'Utbah, the wife of Abu Sufyān, mutilated his body and ate his liver in revenge for her father's death in the Battle of Badr. (*The Life of Muhammad*, Pp. 83, 131, 385).

[27] Ṣafīyah bint 'Abdil-Muṭṭalib was the sister of Ḥamzah and paternal aunt of the Prophet. She was also the mother of az-Zubayr ibn al-'Awwām. (*The Life of Muhammad*, Pp. 387-8 & 513).

of cloth.[28] The narrator, Qutaybah, added, "They were then buried in one grave. Allah's Messenger (ﷺ) asked, "Which of the two knew the most Qur'an?" And the one who knew more was placed in front, facing the *Qiblah*.[29]"

In the case of the martyr, his or her garments are not removed. The shroud is wrapped over the garments in which the person was killed.

5) The number of sheets used to wrap the body can be as few as one sheet, based on Umm 'Aṭīyah's hadith about washing the Prophet's daughter, Zaynab, in which she said,

((فَأَعْطَانَا حِقْوَهُ فَقَالَ: أَشْعِرْنَهَا إِيَّاهُ تَعْنِي إِزَارَهُ))

"He [the Prophet (ﷺ)] threw us his lower wrapper[30] and said, '*Shroud her in it.*'"[31]

It could also be two sheets as in the hadith of the *muḥrim* who was

---

[28] Ibn Taymīyah was of the opinion that they were not literally shrouded in a single sheet of cloth, but that a single sheet was torn and pieces used to shroud two or three bodies individually, even if it did not completely cover them, due to necessity. He argued that if they were in a single sheet, the Prophet (ﷺ) would have asked about the most knowledgeable before shrouding them, to avoid having to undo the shroud and re-shroud them. (*'Awn al-Ma'būd*, vol. 3, p. 165).

[29] Collected by Tirmidhi and Abu Dāwūd (*Sunan Abi Dāwūd*, vol. 2, p. 893, hadith no. 3130) and authenticated by Shaykh al-Albāni in *Ṣaḥīḥ Sunan Abi Dāwūd*, vol. 2, p. 606, hadith no. 2689.

[30] The *izār*, also called a 'waist-wrapper', is a sheet of cloth wrapped around the waist like a skirt. It is called a *lungī* in India and Pakistan, and a *sarong* in Malaysia and Indonesia.

[31] Bukhari (Arabic-English),vol. 2, p. 194, hadith no. 344, Muslim (English trans), vol. 2, p. 445, hadith no. 2041, *Sunan Abi Dāwūd*, vol. 2, Pp. 894-5, hadith no. 3136, *Sunan Ibn Mājah*, vol. 2, p. 372, hadith no. 1458 and *Mishkāt al-Maṣābīḥ*, vol. 1, p. 344.

killed by his horse at ‘Arafah. The Prophet (Blessings and Peace be upon him) said,

((. . . وَكَفِّنُوهُ فِي ثَوْبَيْنِ))

“... and shroud him in two sheets.”[32]

In the case of the male who dies while in a state of *iḥrām*, the two sheets will be the two sheets of his *iḥrām*. Ibn ‘Abbās quoted the Prophet (Blessings and Peace be upon him) as saying,

((أَغْسِلُوا الْمُحْرِمَ فِي ثَوْبَيْهِ اللَّذَيْنِ أَحْرَمَ فِيهِمَا، وَاغْسِلُوهُ بِمَاءٍ وَسِدْرٍ، وَكَفِّنُوهُ فِي ثَوْبَيْهِ))

> *“Wash the muḥrim in the sheets in which he entered the state of iḥrām; wash him with water and lote-tree leaves; and shroud him in his two sheets.”*[33]

The preferable number is generally considered to be three sheets based on the fact that the Prophet (ﷺ) was shrouded in three. However, since the use of one or two sheets were suggested and approved by the Prophet (ﷺ) himself, the Companions’ choice of three sheets cannot be considered more preferable than two or one.

عَنْ عَائِشَةَ رَضِي اللَّهُ عَنْهَا أَنَّ رَسُولَ اللَّهِ ﷺ كُفِّنَ فِي ثَلاَثَةِ أَثْوَابٍ بِيضٍ سَحُولِيَّةٍ لَيْسَ فِيهَا قَمِيصٌ وَلاَ عِمَامَةٌ .

‘Ā’ishah reported that Allah’s Messenger (ﷺ) was shrouded in three sheets of Yemeni cotton cloth from Saḥūl[34] and there was

---

[32] Bukhari (Arabic-English), vol. 2, Pp. 199-200, hadith no. 355, *Ṣaḥīḥ Muslim* vol. 2, p. 596, hadith no. 2746, *Sunan Abi Dāwūd*, vol. 2, p. 920, hadith no. 3232 and *Mishkāt al-Maṣābīḥ*, vol. 1, p. 344.

[33] *Ṣaḥīḥ Sunan an-Nasā’i*, vol. 2, p. 411, hadith no. 1796.

[34] Saḥūl is the name of a town in Yemen (*an-Nihāyah*, vol. 2, p. 347).

not a shirt or a turban[35] among them.

Point of note: There is no difference between the man and woman in the number of sheets used.[36] The Prophet (ﷺ) did not specify a particular number for women and another for men as is commonly held among Muslims today.

6) The preferable colour is white, since Ibn 'Abbās quoted the Messenger of Allah (ﷺ) as saying,

((الْبَسُوا مِنْ ثِيَابِكُمُ الْبَيَاضَ فَإِنَّهَا مِنْ خَيْرِ ثِيَابِكُمْ وَكَفِّنُوا فِيهَا مَوْتَاكُمْ))

"Wear white clothes, for verily it is among the best of your garments and shroud your dead in it also."[37]

It is also recommended that the cloth or at least one of the sheets be striped. Jābir related that the Prophet (Blessings and Peace be upon him) said,

((إِذَا تُوُفِّيَ أَحَدُكُمْ فَوَجَدَ شَيْئًا فَلْيُكَفَّنْ فِي ثَوْبٍ حِبَرَةٍ)).

"If one of you dies and some cloth is available, shroud

---

[35] Collected in all of the six books of hadith. Bukhari (Arabic-English), vol. 2, p. 203, hadith no. 363, Muslim (English trans), vol. 2, p. 447, hadith no. 2052, *Sunan Abi Dāwūd*, vol. 2, p. 896, hadith no. 3145, *Sunan Ibn Mājah*, vol. 2, p. 378, hadith no. 1469, *Muwaṭṭa*, p. 105, hadith no. 516 and *Mishkāt al-Maṣābīḥ*, vol. 1. p. 345,

[36] Laylā bint Qā'if ath-Thaqafīyah's hadith regarding the Prophet's daughter's shroud (used as evidence for the use of five sheets for females) is unauthentic. *Sunan Abi Dāwūd*, vol. 2, p. 897, hadith no. 3151. It is rated unauthentic in *Ḍa'īf Sunan Abi Dāwūd*, p. 319 hadith no. 691 due to the presence in its chain of narration of the narrator, Nūḥ ibn Ḥakīm ath-Thaqafi, about whom nothing is known.

[37] Collected by Abu Dāwūd (*Sunan Abi Dāwūd*, vol. 3, p. 1134 hadith no. 4050), Tirmidhi, Nasā'i and Ibn Mājah (*Sunan Ibn Mājah*, vol. 2, p. 380, hadith no. 1472) and authenticated by Shaykh al-Albāni in *Ṣaḥīḥ Sunan Abi Dāwūd*, vol. 2, p. 766, hadith no. 3426.

him in striped cloth."[38]

7) It is recommended that the shroud be perfumed with incense thrice, except in the case of the *muḥrim,* as was previously mentioned. Jābir quoted the Prophet (ﷺ) as saying,

((إِذَا أَجْمَرْتُمُ الْمَيِّتَ، فَأَجْمِرُوهُ ثَلاَثًا)).

"When you burn incense by your dead, do it three times."[39]

8) Spending large sums of money on the shroud, the way that non-Muslims compete with each other in buying the most expensive coffins, is strictly forbidden in Islam. The sheets should be ordinary cloth, preferably cotton and not synthetics so that it decomposes quickly along with the body and the number of sheets should not exceed three. A noted scholar, Abu aṭ-Ṭayyib, said that if it were not for the fact that the shroud was ordered in Islam primarily to cover the private parts of the body; it would be considered wastage of wealth since it is of no benefit to either the living or the dead. Therefore, both the use of many sheets and expensive cloth should be avoided.[40] Al-Mughīrah ibn Shu'bah reported that the Prophet (ﷺ) said,

((إِنَّ اللَّهَ حَرَّمَ عَلَيْكُمْ عُقُوقَ الأُمَّهَاتِ وَمَنْعًا وَهَاتِ وَوَأْدَ الْبَنَاتِ وَكَرِهَ لَكُمْ قِيلَ وَقَالَ وَكَثْرَةَ السُّؤَالِ وَإِضَاعَةَ الْمَالِ.))

---

[38] Collected by Aḥmad and Abu Dāwūd (*Sunan Abi Dāwūd* vol. 2, p. 896 hadith no. 3144.) and authenticated by Shaykh al-Albāni is *Ṣaḥiḥ Sunan Abi Dawūd*, vol. 2, p. 766, hadith no. 3426.

[39] Collected by Aḥmad (*Musnad Aḥmad*, vol. 3, p. 331), al-Ḥākim, and al-Bayhaqi and authenticated in *Aḥkām al-Janā'iz*, p. 64.

[40] *Ar-Rawḍah an-Nadīyah*, vol. 1, p. 165.

"Verily Allah has forbidden you from harming your mothers, giving and then taking back what you have given, and killing your daughters. And He despises your statements, "It is said" and "he said,"[41] *excessive questioning and wasting your wealth."*[42]

C. Injunctions Concerning the Funeral Procession

1) Following the Bier

To follow a Muslim's bier is among the obligatory rights due to every Muslim from all Muslims who witness his or her funeral procession. Abu Hurayrah reported that the Prophet (ﷺ) said,

((حَقُّ الْمُسْلِمِ عَلَى الْمُسْلِمِ خَمْسٌ رَدُّ السَّلَامِ وَعِيَادَةُ الْمَرِيضِ وَاتِّبَاعُ الْجَنَائِزِ وَإِجَابَةُ الدَّعْوَةِ وَتَشْمِيتُ الْعَاطِسِ)).

"Every Muslim has five rights due to him from his fellow Muslims: Returning his greetings of salām (peace), visiting him when he is sick, following his bier, accepting his invitation (for food), and praying for his well being when he sneezes[43]*."*[44]

---

[41] These are the introductory statements for gossip.

[42] Bukhari (Arabic-English), vol. 8, p. 6 hadith no. 6, Muslim (English trans), vol. 3, p. 929 hadith no. 4257 and *Mishkāt al-Maṣābīḥ*,, vol. 2, Pp. 1024-25.

[43] By saying: *Yarḥamukal-lāh* (may Allah have mercy on you).

[44] Bukhari (Arabic-English), vol. 2, Pp. 187-88, hadith no. 332, Muslim (English trans), vol. 3, p. 1183, hadith no. 5378, *Sunan Abi Dāwūd*, vol. 3, p. 1398, hadith no. 5012, *Sunan Ibn Mājah*, vol. 2, p. 360, hadith no. 1435 and *Mishkāt al-Maṣābīḥ*, vol. 1, p. 320.

This practice is recommended because it helps to keep Muslims in touch with the reality of death and the after-life. The believers all need to be reminded about death from time to time, because the material needs, pleasures, and distractions of this life easily cause humans to forget about the life to come. Abu Sa'īd reported that the Prophet (ﷺ) said,

((عُودُوا الْمَرِيْضَ، وَاتَّبِعُوا الْجَنَائِزَ، تُذَكِّرُكُمُ الآخِرَةَ))

"Visit the sick and follow the biers, for it reminds you of the next life."[45]

2) Method of Following the Bier

There are two basic ways of following the bier:

a) Following it from the family's home until the funeral prayer is made for the deceased.

b) Following it from the family's home until the body has been buried.

Both ways were done by the Prophet (ﷺ), but he favoured the second method by indicating that its reward was greater. Abu Hurayrah quoted him as saying,

((مَنْ شَهِدَ الْجَنَازَةَ حَتَّى يُصَلِّيَ فَلَهُ قِيرَاطٌ وَمَنْ شَهِدَ حَتَّى تُدْفَنَ كَانَ لَهُ قِيرَاطَانِ قِيلَ وَمَا الْقِيرَاطَانِ قَالَ مِثْلُ الْجَبَلَيْنِ الْعَظِيمَيْنِ)).

"Whoever follows a Muslim's bier, out of Eemān and seeking to increase his account of good deeds, until he makes the funeral prayer for it will have a Qīrāṭ's worth of reward. And whoever follows it until it is buried, will

[45] Collected by Bukhari (*al-Adab al-Mufrad*, p. 75) and Aḥmad (*Musnad Aḥmad*, vol. 3, p. 27) and authenticated in *Aḥkām al-Janā'iz*, Pp. 66-7.

get two Qīrāṭs" He was then asked what two Qīrāṭs were and he replied, "They are equivalent to two huge mountains; (the smaller of the two is like Mount Uḥud)[46]."

3) The Participation of Women

The virtue of following the bier is basically for men alone. Women are not encouraged to take part, based on the fact that the Prophet (ﷺ) prohibited their participation. However, his prohibition was one of dislike rather than absolute forbiddance as is evident from the following narration of a female Companion of the Prophet.

عَنْ أُمِّ عَطِيَّةَ رَضِيَ اللَّهُ عَنْهَا قَالَتْ: نُهِينَا عَنِ اتِّبَاعِ الْجَنَائِزِ وَلَمْ يُعْزَمْ عَلَيْنَا.

Umm 'Aṭīyah said, "*(Allah's Messenger) forbade us from following the bier, but he did not demand that we obey.*"[47]

The crowds which often follow funeral processions and the close contact associated with it represent an unsuitable circumstance for women. Where the crowds are absent and women can follow the bier without being pushed and trodden upon, they may take part in the funeral procession.

---

[46] Reported by Abu Hurayrah and collected in all the six books of hadith. Bukhari (Arabic-English), vol. 2, p. 230, hadith no. 410, Muslim (English trans), vol. 2, Pp. 449-50, hadith no. 2067, *Sunan Abi Dāwūd*, vol. 2, p. 900, hadith no. 3162, *Sunan Ibn Mājah*, vol. 2, Pp. 414-5, hadith no. 1539 and *Mishkāt al-Maṣābīḥ*, vol. 1, Pp. 347-48. The addition in brackets is found in Muslim's narration.

[47] Bukhari (Arabic-English), vol. 2, p. 206, hadith no. 368, Muslim (English trans), vol. 2, p. 445, hadith no. 2039, *Sunan Abi Dāwūd*, vol. 2, Pp. 899-900, hadith no. 3161 and *Sunan Ibn Mājah*, vol. 2, p. 434, hadith no. 1577.

4) The dirge[48]

Following the bier with wailing, chants, dirges, burning incense etc., are all forbidden and considered *bid'ah* (religious innovation). The way of the Prophet (ﷺ) and his Companions was to maintain silence while walking with the bier. Silence at this time allows those present to contemplate the realities of life and death and extract real lessons from their participation.[49] Abu Hurayrah reported that the Prophet (ﷺ) said,

((لاَ تُتْبَعُ الْجَنَازَةُ بِصَوْتٍ وَلاَ نَارٍ))

"*Do not follow the bier with voice or fire.*"[50]

This prohibition includes *dhikr* (chants using Allah's names or attributes). Qays ibn 'Ibād said that the Companions of the Prophet (ﷺ) used to despise loud voices near the bier.[51] It is also the practice of some religions and cultures to make a lot of noise during the funeral procession and Muslims are instructed to avoid imitation of all the religious and cultural practices of other nations.

5) Haste in Carrying the Bier

The pallbearers[52] are required to walk quickly from the deceased's house to the masjid and from the masjid to the graveyard. The Prophet (ﷺ) is reported by Abu Hurayrah to have said,

---

48 A song sung at a burial or for a dead person.

49 *Al-Adhkār,* p. 203.

50 *Sunan Abi Dāwūd*, vol. 2, p. 900, hadith no. 3165 and *Sunan Ibn Mājah*, vol. 2, p. 387 hadith no. 1487, vol. 2, p. 437 hadith no. 1583.

51 Collected by al-Bayhaqi and authenticated in *Aḥkām al-Janā'iz*, p. 71.

52 Those carrying the bier.

((أَسْرِعُوا بِالْجِنَازَةِ فَإِنْ تَكُ صَالِحَةً فَخَيْرٌ تُقَدِّمُونَهَا وَإِنْ يَكُ سِوَى ذَلِكَ فَشَرٌّ تَضَعُونَهُ عَنْ رِقَابِكُمْ)).

"Hasten with the bier for if the deceased was righteous, what you are taking him to is good for him, and if he was not then, you are removing evil from your necks."[53]

6) Accompanying the Bier

Those walking with the bier are allowed to walk in front, behind, or on either side of it, while those riding should be behind it. Al-Mughīrah narrated that the Prophet (Blessings and Peace be upon him) said,

((الرَّاكِبُ يَسِيرُ خَلْفَ الْجَنَازَةِ وَالْمَاشِي يَمْشِي خَلْفَهَا وَأَمَامَهَا وَعَنْ يَمِينِهَا وَعَنْ يَسَارِهَا قَرِيبًا مِنْهَا)).

"The rider should go behind the bier while those on foot can walk behind it, in front of it, on its right and on its left, keeping near to it."[54]

عَنْ سَالِمٍ عَنْ أَبِيهِ قَالَ رَأَيْتُ النَّبِيَّ ﷺ وَأَبَا بَكْرٍ وَعُمَرَ يَمْشُونَ أَمَامَ الْجَنَازَةِ.

[53] Collected in all of the six books of hadith. Bukhari (Arabic-English), vol. 2, p. 225, hadith no. 401, Muslim (English trans), vol. 2, p. 448, hadith no. 2059, *Sunan Abi Dāwūd*, vol. 2, p. 903, hadith no. 3175, *Sunan Ibn Mājah*, vol. 2, p. 382, hadith no. 1477, *Muwaṭṭa*, p. 115, hadith no. 570 and *Mishkāt al-Maṣābīḥ*, vol. 1, p. 347.

[54] Collected by the authors of the four *Sunans*. *Sunan Abi Dāwūd*, vol. 2, p. 902, hadith no. 3174, *Sunan Ibn Mājah*, vol. 2, p. 384, hadith no. 1481 and *Mishkāt al-Maṣābīḥ*, vol. 1, Pp. 350-1. It is authenticated by Shaykh al-Albāni in *Ṣaḥīḥ Sunan Abi Dāwūd,* vol. 2, p. 612, hadith no. 2723.

Sālim[55] quoted his father as saying that he saw the Prophet (ﷺ), Abu Bakr, and 'Umar all walk in front of the bier.[56]

عَنْ أَنَسِ ابْنِ مَالِكٍ قَالَ: إِنَّ رَسُولَ اللَّهِ ﷺ وَأَبَا بَكْرٍ وَعُمَرَ كَانُوا يَمْشُونَ أَمَامَ الْجَنَازَةِ وَخَلْفَهُ.

Anas ibn Mālik related that Allah's Messenger (ﷺ), Abu Bakr, and 'Umar all used to walk in front of the bier and behind it.[57]

However, it is preferable to walk behind the bier based on the many prophetic statements in which he told his followers to 'follow' the bier. The preference for walking behind the bier is also supported by a statement from 'Ali ibn Abi Ṭālib in which he is reported to have said, "Walking behind the bier is superior to walking in front of it, like the superiority of a man's prayer in congregation over his prayer alone."[58]

7) Standing for the Bier

In the early days of Islam, the Prophet (ﷺ) used to stand when the

---

[55] Sālim ibn 'Abdullah ibn 'Umar was one of the great scholars among the *tābi'īn*. Aḥmad ibn Ḥanbal and Isḥāq ibn Rāḥaway considered the reports of az-Zuhri from Sālim from his father to be the most authentic of isnāds. See *Tah-dhīb at-Tah-dhīb* in *Maktabah al-Hadith ash-Sharīf* CD, *Kutub ar-Rijāl, man ismuhū Sābiq wa Sālim.*

[56] *Sunan Abi Dāwūd*, vol. 2, p. 902, hadith no. 3173, *Sunan Ibn Mājah*, vol. 2, p. 384, hadith no. 1482, *Muwaṭṭa*, p. 106, hadith no. 520 and *Mishkāt al-Maṣābīḥ*, vol. 1, p. 351. It is authenticated by Shaykh al-Albāni in *Ṣaḥīḥ Sunan Abi Dāwūd*, vol. 2, p. 612, hadith no. 2722.

[57] Collected by aṭ-Ṭaḥāwī (1/278) and authenticated in *Aḥkām al-Janā'iz*, Pp. 73-74.

[58] Collected by Ibn Abi Shaybah in *al-Musannaf*, vol. 4, hadith no. 101, aṭ-Ṭaḥāwī (1/279), al-Bayhaqi (4/25), and Aḥmad (754) and authenticated in *Aḥkām al-Janā'iz*, p. 74.

bier passed by, but he later abolished it. Wāqid ibn 'Amr said, "I witnessed a bier of the Salamah tribe so I stood up until Nāfi' ibn Jubayr said, "Sit down and I will give you some reliable information on this matter." (When I sat down, he said), "Mas'ūd ibn al-Ḥakam az-Zarqi told me that he heard 'Ali ibn Abi Ṭālib in Kūfah Square say,

((كَانَ رَسُولُ اللَّهِ ﷺ أَمَرَنَا بِالْقِيَامِ فِي الْجِنَازَةِ ثُمَّ جَلَسَ بَعْدَ ذَلِكَ وَأَمَرَنَا بِالْجُلُوسِ)).

"*Allah's Messenger used to order us to stand for the bier at first, then later he used to sit and ordered us to sit also.*"[59]

8) Transporting the Bier

Transportation of the bier in a funeral coach or vehicle (hearse) according to the traditions of non-Muslims is forbidden. Carts which could have been used to transport the dead existed in the Prophet's time, but he instructed his followers to walk and carry the bier with their own hands. The Prophet (Blessings and Peace be upon him) explicitly instructed his followers on numerous occasions to differ in their religious and social customs from non-Muslims.[60] For example:

عَنِ ابْنِ عُمَرَ قَالَ: قَالَ رَسُولُ اللَّهِ ﷺ: ((مَنْ تَشَبَّهَ بِقَوْمٍ فَهُوَ مِنْهُمْ)).

---

[59] Collected by Aḥmad, al-Bayhaqi and Ibn Ḥibbān. See also Muslim (English trans), vol. 2, Pp. 455-6, hadith nos. 2099 & 2100, *Sunan Abi Dāwūd*, vol. 2, p. 901 hadith no. 3169, *Sunan Ibn Mājah*, vol. 2, p. 417, hadith no. 1544, *Muwaṭṭa*, p. 110, hadith no. 545 and *Mishkāt al-Maṣābīḥ*, vol. 1, p. 353.

[60] Al-Albāni collected most of the narrations prohibiting imitation in his book *Ḥijāb al-Mar'ah al-Muslimah fil-Kitāb was-Sunnah*.

Ibn 'Umar quoted Allah's Messenger (Blessings and Peace be upon him) as saying, "*Whoever imitates a people becomes one of them.*"[61]

The Prophet (ﷺ) also warned his followers against imitating others by prophesying that future generations of Muslims would imitate the practices of other religious groups and customs of other nations.

عَنْ أَبِي سَعِيدٍ أَنَّ النَّبِيَّ ﷺ قَالَ : ((لَتَتَّبِعُنَّ سَنَنَ مَنْ قَبْلَكُمْ شِبْرًا بِشِبْرٍ وَذِرَاعًا بِذِرَاعٍ حَتَّى لَوْ سَلَكُوا جُحْرَ ضَبٍّ لَسَلَكْتُمُوهُ)) قُلْنَا يَا رَسُولَ اللَّهِ الْيَهُودَ وَالنَّصَارَى؟ قَالَ: ((فَمَنْ ؟))

Abu Sa'īd al-Khudri related that the Prophet (ﷺ) said, "*You will follow the ways of those nations who were before you, inch by inch, yard by yard, so much so that if they entered a lizard's hole, you would follow them.*" We asked, "O Messenger of Allah, (do you mean) the Jews and Christians?" He replied, "*(If not them) who else?*[62]" In another narration by Abu Hurayrah in which the Prophet (ﷺ) made a similar statement about following the customs of other people, his Companions asked, "O Messenger of Allah, (do you mean people) like those of Persia and Rome?" He replied, "*Who are the people besides them?*"[63]

Furthermore, the Prophet's instruction to follow the bier becomes difficult, if not impossible, when the beir is transported in a vehicle, and the goal of remembering the next life is often lost as

---

[61] *Sunan Abi Dāwūd*, vol. 3, p. 1127, hadith no. 4020 and authenticated by Shaykh al-Albāni in *Ṣaḥīḥ Sunan Abi Dāwūd*, vol. 2, p. 761, hadith no. 3401.

[62] Bukhari (Arabic-English), vol. 9, Pp. 314-5, hadith no. 422 and Muslim (English trans), vol. 4, p. 1403, hadith no. 6448.

[63] Bukhari (Arabic-English), vol. 9, p. 314, hadith no. 421.

people are distanced from the dead. Al-Mughīrah narrated that the Prophet (ﷺ) said,

> *"The rider should go behind the bier while those on foot can walk behind it, in front of it, on its right and on its left, keeping near to it."*[64]

In countries where Muslims are a relatively new minority, like America, England, France and Germany, where there are virtually no Muslim neighbourhoods with mosques and Muslim graveyards nearby, the use of motorized transportation for part of the funeral procession is unavoidable. In fact, in some of these countries, the laws specify that a hearse must be used to transport the dead. Such circumstances represent exceptions to the general rule. However, Muslims in these lands should still try their utmost to avoid imitation to whatever degree they can.

---

[64] Collected by the authors of the four *Sunans*. *Sunan Abi Dāwūd*, vol. 2, p. 902, hadith no. 3174, *Sunan Ibn Mājah*, vol. 2, p. 384, hadith no. 1481 and *Mishkāt al-Maṣābīḥ*, vol. 1, Pp. 350-1. It is authenticated by Shaykh al-Albāni in *Ṣaḥīḥ Sunan Abi Dāwūd*, vol. 2, p. 612, hadith no. 2723.

people [illegible] the dead [illegible] the Prophet [illegible]

[illegible]

In countries where Muslims are a relatively small minority, like America, England, France and Germany, [illegible] virtually no Muslim neighbourhoods with [illegible] graveyards [illegible] the use of motor [illegible] part of the funeral procession is unavoidable. In [illegible] these countries the laws specify that [illegible] must be used to transport the dead. Such circumstances represent [illegible] the general rule. However, Muslims in those [illegible] should still do their utmost to avoid imitation to whatever degree [illegible]

[illegible] Collected by two authors of the four Sunan [illegible] 902, [illegible] *Sunan* [illegible] and [illegible] Vol. 1, pp. 1504. It is authentic [illegible] Shaykh al-Albani in *Sahih Sunan* [illegible] vol.2, p. 4[illegible]

CHAPTER 4: FUNERAL PRAYER

A. Injunctions Concerning the Prayer

1) *Farḍ Kifāyah* (A Communal Duty)

The performance of *Ṣalātul-Janāzah* (the funeral prayer) is considered *farḍ kifāyah*. If a Muslim is buried without it being performed, the whole Muslim community is held responsible, but as long as some people gather and perform it, the obligation is removed from the community as a whole.

Exceptions

A Child Below the Age of Puberty

A child born dead or aborted after the fourth month, or one that dies before reaching puberty, does not require a funeral prayer because the Prophet (ﷺ) did not perform the prayer for his own son. This fact is borne out by 'Ā'ishah's statement,

عَنْ عَائِشَةَ قَالَتْ: ((مَاتَ إِبْرَاهِيمُ بْنُ النَّبِيِّ ﷺ وَهُوَ ابْنُ ثَمَانِيَةَ عَشَرَ شَهْرًا فَلَمْ يُصَلِّ عَلَيْهِ رَسُولُ اللَّهِ ﷺ)).

"The Prophet's son Ibrāhīm died when he was eighteen months old and the Prophet (ﷺ) did not make *ṣalāh* for him."[1]

---

[1] *Sunan Abi Dāwūd*, vol. 2, p. 905, hadith no. 3181 and authenticated by Shaykh al-Albāni in *Ṣaḥīḥ Sunan Abi Dāwūd*, vol. 2, p. 614, hadith no. 2730.

Although the funeral prayer is not *farḍ* (compulsory) in this case, it is still legally a part of the *Sharī'ah*, recommended and the Prophet (ﷺ) performed it other occasions. For example, al-Mughīrah ibn Shu'bah reported that the Prophet (ﷺ) said,

((وَالسِّقْطُ يُصَلَّى عَلَيْهِ وَيُدْعَى لِوَالِدَيْهِ بِالْمَغْفِرَةِ وَالرَّحْمَةِ)).

> *"Ṣalāh is made for the aborted child and forgiveness and mercy are asked for his parents."*[2]

'Ā'ishah also reported that a dead child from the Anṣār was brought to the Prophet (ﷺ) and he led the funeral prayers for him.[3]

A Child Aborted Before the Fourth Month

If the child was aborted before the fourth month, no funeral prayer is performed for it since it was not considered living, in the human sense that it has a soul which may be prayed for.[4] This ruling is based on the hadith related by Ibn Mas'ūd in which the Prophet (ﷺ) is quoted as saying,

((إِنَّ أَحَدَكُمْ يُجْمَعُ فِي بَطْنِ أُمِّهِ أَرْبَعِينَ يَوْمًا ثُمَّ يَكُونُ عَلَقَةً مِثْلَ ذَلِكَ ثُمَّ يَكُونُ مُضْغَةً مِثْلَ ذَلِكَ ثُمَّ يَبْعَثُ اللَّهُ إِلَيْهِ مَلَكًا بِأَرْبَعِ كَلِمَاتٍ فَيُكْتَبُ عَمَلُهُ وَأَجَلُهُ وَرِزْقُهُ وَشَقِيٌّ أَوْ سَعِيدٌ ثُمَّ يُنْفَخُ فِيهِ الرُّوحُ)).

> *"Indeed the creation of each of you comes together in his mother's womb for forty days, after which he*

[2] *Sunan Abi Dāwūd*, vol. 2, p. 902, hadith no. 3174, *Sunan Ibn Mājah*, vol. 2, p. 398 hadith no. 1507 and *Mishkāt al-Maṣābīḥ*, vol. 1, p. 350 and authenticated by Shaykh al-Albāni in *Ṣaḥīḥ Sunan Abi Dāwūd*, vol. 2, p. 612, hadith no. 2723.

[3] Muslim (English trans), vol. 4, p. 1400, hadith no. 6436 and *Sunan Ibn Mājah*, vol. 1, Pp. 48-9, hadith no. 82.

[4] *Aḥkām al-Janā'iz*, p. 81.

becomes a leach-like clot for a similar period, then he becomes a clump of chewed flesh for a similar period. Following that, Allah sends an angel to him with four records and writes his deeds, his life span, his provisions, and whether he will be wretched or happy, and then he blows the soul into him."[5]

The Martyr (*Shahīd*)

Ṣalātul-Janāzah is also not required for a *shahīd*, one who dies or is killed while fighting for the cause of Islam. Such an individual can be buried without *Ṣalātul-Janāzah* as was mentioned earlier in the case of the martyrs of the Battle of Uḥud. However, the funeral prayer may be performed for martyrs since the Prophet (ﷺ) did perform *Ṣalātul-Janāzah* for those who died in battle on other occasions.

عَنْ شَدَّادِ بْنِ الْهَادِ أَنَّ رَجُلاً مِنَ ٱلأَعْرَابِ جَاءَ إِلَى النَّبِى ﷺ فَآمَنَ بِهِ وَاتَّبَعَهُ ثُمَّ قَالَ أُهَاجِرُ مَعَكَ فَلَبِثُوا قَلِيلاً ثُمَّ نَهَضُوا فِي قِتَالِ الْعَدُوِّ فَأُتِيَ بِهِ النَّبِيُّ ﷺ يُحْمَلُ قَدْ أَصَابَهُ سَهْمٌ ثُمَّ كَفَّنَهُ النَّبِيُّ ﷺ فِي جُبَّةِ النَّبِيِّ ﷺ ثُمَّ قَدَّمَهُ فَصَلَّى عَلَيْهِ.

Shaddād ibn al-Hād reported that a Bedouin came to the Prophet (ﷺ) and accepted Islam. Then he made *Hijrah* along with the Prophet (ﷺ) and stayed in Madīnah for a short time before going out to fight the enemy. (During the battle) he was killed by an arrow and his body was brought to the Prophet (ﷺ). The Prophet (ﷺ) shrouded him in his own cloak, put his body in the front, and

[5] Bukhari (Arabic-English), vol. 8, p. 387, hadith no. 593 and Muslim (English trans), vol. 4, p. 1391, hadith no. 6390.

led the funeral prayer for him."[6]

2) An Executed Criminal

If one voluntarily confesses to a crime deserving the death sentence, according to Islamic law, he should be prayed for this is due to the fact that such a confession is an unparalleled form of true repentance.

عَنْ عِمْرَانَ بْنِ حُصَيْنٍ أَنَّ امْرَأَةً مِنْ جُهَيْنَةَ أَتَتْ نَبِيَّ اللَّهِ ﷺ وَهِيَ حُبْلَى مِنَ الزِّنَى فَقَالَتْ يَا نَبِيَّ اللَّهِ أَصَبْتُ حَدًّا فَأَقِمْهُ عَلَيَّ فَدَعَا نَبِيُّ اللَّهِ ﷺ وَلِيَّهَا فَقَالَ : ((أَحْسِنْ إِلَيْهَا فَإِذَا وَضَعَتْ فَأْتِنِي بِهَا)) فَفَعَلَ فَأَمَرَ بِهَا نَبِيُّ اللَّهِ ﷺ فَشُكَّتْ عَلَيْهَا ثِيَابُهَا ثُمَّ أَمَرَ بِهَا فَرُجِمَتْ ثُمَّ صَلَّى عَلَيْهَا فَقَالَ لَهُ عُمَرُ تُصَلِّي عَلَيْهَا يَا نَبِيَّ اللَّهِ وَقَدْ زَنَتْ فَقَالَ : ((لَقَدْ تَابَتْ تَوْبَةً لَوْ قُسِمَتْ بَيْنَ سَبْعِينَ مِنْ أَهْلِ الْمَدِينَةِ لَوَسِعَتْهُمْ)).

'Imrān ibn Ḥuṣayn reported that a woman pregnant by adultery, from the Juhaynah tribe came to the Prophet (ﷺ) and said, "I have committed a capital offense so apply the law to me." The Prophet (ﷺ) called her guardian and said, *"Treat her well, and when she delivers bring her back to me."* When he brought her back, the Prophet (ﷺ) ordered that her clothes be drawn tightly around her. Then he ordered that she be stoned to death. After that he led the funeral prayers for her. 'Umar asked him, "Will you pray for her, O Prophet of Allah, even though she committed adultery?" The Prophet (ﷺ) replied,

> *"Certainly, her repentance was so great that if it were divided up among seventy residents of Madīnah, it*

[6] *Ṣaḥīḥ Sunan an-Nasā'i*, vol. 2, p. 420, hadith no. 1845. See also *Aḥkām al-Janā'iz*, Pp. 62 and 82.

would have been more than enough for all of them."[7]

3) The Corrupt

The funeral prayer should be held even for those known to be involved in corruption, like alcholics, drug addicts, adulterers, and those who abandoned prayer and Zakāh, while acknowledging that both are compulsory duties.[8] However, it is preferable that the scholars and pious do not join in their funeral prayer as a punishment for them and deterrent for others like them. The Prophet's practice was to refrain from praying for those who committed major sins, although he did allow others to do so. Abu Qatādah said,

كَانَ رَسُولِ اللَّهِ ﷺ إِذَا دُعِيَ لِجَنَازَةٍ سَأَلَ عَنْهَا، فَإِنْ أُثْنِيَ عَلَيْهَا خَيْرٌ قَامَ فَصَلَّى عَلَيْهَا، وَإِنْ أُثْنِيَ عَلَيْهَا غَيْرُ ذَلِكَ قَالَ لِأَهْلِهَا: ((شَأْنُكُمْ بِهَا))، وَلَمْ يُصَلِّ عَلَيْهَا.

"If the Messenger of Allah (ﷺ) was invited to lead a funeral prayer, he would ask about the dead person. If good was said about the person, he would get up and lead the prayer. But if other than that were said, he would tell the family, "*It is your affair to deal with*," and he would not take part in the funeral prayer for that person.[9]

---

[7] Muslim (English trans), vol. 3, p. 917, hadith no. 4207, *Sunan Abi Dāwūd*, vol. 3, Pp. 1237-38, hadith no. 4426, *Mishkāt al-Maṣābīḥ*, vol. 1, Pp. 759-760 and *Riyadh-uṣ-Ṣaleḥīn*, vol. 1, p. 27, hadith no. 22.

[8] Those who deny that prayer or zakāh is obligatory become disbelievers, in which case no funeral prayer may be held for them and they should not be buried among Muslims (i.e. in a non-Muslim graveyard).

[9] Collected in *Musnad Aḥmad*, vol. 5, p. 399 and *al-Mustadrak*, vol. 1, p. 374 and authenticated in *Aḥkām al-Janā'iz*, p. 84.

جَابِرُ بْنُ سَمُرَةَ قَالَ مَرِضَ رَجُلٌ فَصِيحَ عَلَيْهِ فَجَاءَ جَارُهُ إِلَى رَسُولِ اللَّهِ ﷺ فَقَالَ لَهُ إِنَّهُ قَدْ مَاتَ قَالَ: ((وَمَا يُدْرِيكَ؟)) قَالَ: أَنَا رَأَيْتُهُ قَالَ رَسُولُ اللَّهِ ﷺ: ((إِنَّهُ لَمْ يَمُتْ)) قَالَ فَرَجَعَ فَصِيحَ عَلَيْهِ فَجَاءَ إِلَى رَسُولِ اللَّهِ ﷺ فَقَالَ إِنَّهُ قَدْ مَاتَ فَقَالَ النَّبِيُّ ﷺ: ((إِنَّهُ لَمْ يَمُتْ)) فَرَجَعَ فَصِيحَ عَلَيْهِ فَقَالَتِ امْرَأَتُهُ انْطَلِقْ إِلَى رَسُولِ اللَّهِ ﷺ فَأَخْبِرْهُ فَقَالَ الرَّجُلُ اللَّهُمَّ الْعَنْهُ قَالَ ثُمَّ انْطَلَقَ الرَّجُلُ فَرَآهُ قَدْ نَحَرَ نَفْسَهُ بِمِشْقَصٍ مَعَهُ فَانْطَلَقَ إِلَى النَّبِيِّ ﷺ فَأَخْبَرَهُ أَنَّهُ قَدْ مَاتَ فَقَالَ: ((وَمَا يُدْرِيكَ؟)) قَالَ رَأَيْتُهُ يَنْحَرُ نَفْسَهُ بِمَشَاقِصَ مَعَهُ قَالَ: ((أَنْتَ رَأَيْتَهُ؟)) قَالَ: نَعَمْ قَالَ: ((إِذًا لاَ أُصَلِّيَ عَلَيْهِ)).

Jābir ibn Samurah reported that when a man got very sick and his family began screaming, his neighbour went to the Prophet (ﷺ) and told him that the man had died. The Prophet (ﷺ) asked him what made him think so and he replied that he had seen him. The Prophet (ﷺ) then told him that he was not yet dead. When he returned, the man's family again screamed and his wife told the neighbour to go and inform the Prophet (ﷺ). The neighbour asked Allah to curse the man and then went to look at him. He found, that he killed himself with a broad blade, so he went and informed the Prophet (ﷺ) that he was dead. When the Prophet (ﷺ) asked him how he knew, he described what he had witnessed. The Prophet (ﷺ) then asked the neighbour if he saw the dead man with his own eyes and when he replied that he had, the Prophet (ﷺ) then said, "*In that case, I will not pray for him.*"[10]

---

[10] Muslim (English trans), vol. 2, p. 464, hadith no. 2133, *Sunan Abi Dāwūd*, vol. 2, hadith no. 3179, Pp. 903-4 (the wording in his version) and *Sunan Ibn Mājah*, vol. 2, p. 408, hadith no. 1526.

4) Debtors

In the beginning, the Prophet (ﷺ) refused to lead the funeral prayers for those who died owing debts and had no means to repay them. This was done to emphasize the importance of clearing one's debts. However, he later led prayers for them and paid off their debts from the charity (*ṣadaqah*) which he received.

عَنْ أَبِي هُرَيْرَةَ أَنَّ رَسُولَ اللَّهِ ﷺ كَانَ يُؤْتَى بِالرَّجُلِ الْمَيِّتِ عَلَيْهِ الدَّيْنُ فَيَسْأَلُ هَلْ تَرَكَ لِدَيْنِهِ مِنْ قَضَاءٍ فَإِنْ حُدِّثَ أَنَّهُ تَرَكَ وَفَاءً صَلَّى عَلَيْهِ وَإِلاَّ قَالَ : ((صَلُّوا عَلَى صَاحِبِكُمْ)) فَلَمَّا فَتَحَ اللَّهُ عَلَيْهِ الْفُتُوحَ قَالَ: ((أَنَا أَوْلَى بِالْمُؤْمِنِينَ مِنْ أَنْفُسِهِمْ فَمَنْ تُوُفِّيَ وَعَلَيْهِ دَيْنٌ فَعَلَيَّ قَضَاؤُهُ وَمَنْ تَرَكَ مَالاً فَهُوَ لِوَرَثَتِهِ)).

Abu Hurayrah related that when the dead body of a person owing debts was brought to Allah's Messenger (ﷺ), he would ask whether he had left enough property to clear his debt. If the property left was sufficient, the Prophet (ﷺ) would lead the funeral prayer for him, otherwise (he would not, and) he would tell his Companions, "*Do the prayers for your Companion.*" When Allah opened the gateways of victory for him, he said,

> *"I am closer to the believers than their own selves*[11] *so if anyone dies leaving a debt, its payment is my responsibility, and if anyone leaves a property, it goes to his heirs."*[12]

---

[11] This statement is in reference to verse 6 of chapter *al-Aḥzāb* (33):

﴿النَّبِيُّ أَوْلَى بِالْمُؤْمِنِينَ مِنْ أَنْفُسِهِمْ﴾

﴾The Prophet is closer to the believers than their own selves.﴿

[12] Muslim (English trans), vol. 3, p. 855, hadith no. 3944.

5) Burial without *Ṣalāh*

It is allowable to perform the funeral prayer by the grave of someone who was buried without *Ṣalātul-Janāzah* being performed for him.

عَنِ ابْنِ عَبَّاسٍ قَالَ: مَاتَ إِنْسَانٌ كَانَ رَسُولُ اللَّهِ ﷺ يَعُودُهُ فَمَاتَ بِاللَّيْلِ فَدَفَنُوهُ لَيْلاً فَلَمَّا أَصْبَحَ أَخْبَرُوهُ فَقَالَ: ((مَا مَنَعَكُمْ أَنْ تُعْلِمُونِي ؟)) قَالُوا كَانَ اللَّيْلُ وَكَانَتْ ظُلْمَةٌ فَكَرِهْنَا أَنْ نَشُقَّ عَلَيْكَ فَأَتَى قَبْرَهُ فَصَلَّى عَلَيْهِ.

Ibn 'Abbās reported that a man whom the Prophet (ﷺ) used to visit died and they buried him at night. In the morning when they informed the Prophet (ﷺ), he asked what prevented them from informing him (earlier) and they replied that they did not want to place only unnecessary burden on him. The Prophet (ﷺ) then went with them to his grave and led them in a funeral prayer for him.[13]

6) *Ṣalātul-Ghā'ib*

If someone dies in a country or situation where there is no one to perform the *Ṣalātul-Janāzah* for him, it is permitted for a group of Muslims to make a funeral prayer for him in his absence. This prayer is known as *Ṣalātul-Ghā'ib*.

عَنْ أَبِي هُرَيْرَةَ قَالَ نَعَى رَسُولُ اللَّهِ ﷺ النَّجَاشِيَّ لِأَصْحَابِهِ وَهُوَ بِالْمَدِينَةِ فَصَفُّوا خَلْفَهُ وَصَلَّى عَلَيْهِ.

---

[13] Bukhari (Arabic-English), vol. 2, p. 192, hadith no. 339, p. 228, hadith no. 407, Muslim (English trans), vol. 2, p. 453, hadith no. 2084, *Sunan Abi Dāwūd*, vol. 2, Pp. 910-11, hadith no. 3197, *Sunan Ibn Mājah*, vol. 2, Pp. 410-11, hadith no. 1530 and *Mishkāt al-Maṣābīḥ*, vol. 1, p. 349.

Abu Hurayrah reported that when Allah's Messenger (ﷺ) announced the death of the Najāshi[14] to his Companions while (they were) in Madīnah, they lined up behind him and prayed (the funeral prayer) for him.[15]

7) Disbelievers

The performance of funeral prayers or even seeking forgiveness or mercy for those who die in open disbelief or *Nifāq* (subtle disbelief) is strictly forbidden based on the following instruction of Allah in the Qur'an:

﴿وَلَا تُصَلِّ عَلَىٰٓ أَحَدٍ مِّنْهُم مَّاتَ أَبَدًا وَلَا تَقُمْ عَلَىٰ قَبْرِهِۦٓ ۖ إِنَّهُمْ كَفَرُوا۟
بِٱللَّهِ وَرَسُولِهِۦ وَمَاتُوا۟ وَهُمْ فَـٰسِقُونَ ﴿٨٤﴾﴾ (سورة التوبة ٩ : ٨٧)

﴾Never pray for any of them who die, and do not stand by their graves, for verily they have disbelieved in Allah and His Messenger and died in sin.﴿ (Qur'an 9: 84)

This verse was revealed when the Prophet (ﷺ) prayed the funeral prayer for 'Abdullah ibn Ubayy, the leader of the hypocrites of Madīnah.

عَنِ ابْنِ عُمَرَ قَالَ جَاءَ عَبْدُ اللَّهِ بْنُ عَبْدِ اللَّهِ بْنِ أُبَيٍّ إِلَى النَّبِيِّ ﷺ حِينَ مَاتَ أَبُوهُ فَقَالَ أَعْطِنِي قَمِيصَكَ أُكَفِّنْهُ فِيهِ وَصَلِّ عَلَيْهِ وَاسْتَغْفِرْ لَهُ

---

[14] 'Negus' (Ar. Najāshi) was the title of the Ethiopian ruler with whom a group of eighty-three Muslims from Makkah sought refuge prior to their migration to Madīnah. He converted to Islam after listening to a reading of Chapter 19 from the Qur'an (*The Life of Muhammad*, Pp. 146-155).

[15] Bukhari (Arabic-English), vol. 2, p. 191 hadith no. 337, Muslim (English trans), vol. 2, p. 452, hadith no. 2082, *Sunan Abi Dāwūd*, vol. 2, p. 911 hadith no. 3198, *Sunan Ibn Mājah*, vol. 2, p. 412, hadith no. 1534 and p. 413 hadith no. 1535 and *Mishkāt al-Maṣābīḥ*, vol. 1, p. 348.

فَأَعْطَاهُ قَمِيصَهُ وَقَالَ إِذَا فَرَغْتُمْ فَآذِنُونِي فَلَمَّا أَرَادَ أَنْ يُصَلِّيَ جَذَبَهُ عُمَرُ وَقَالَ أَلَيْسَ قَدْ نَهَى اللَّهُ أَنْ تُصَلِّيَ عَلَى الْمُنَافِقِينَ فَقَالَ: ((أَنَا بَيْنَ خِيرَتَيْنِ: اسْتَغْفِرْ لَهُمْ أَوْ لاَ تَسْتَغْفِرْ لَهُمْ)) فَصَلَّى عَلَيْهِ فَأَنْزَلَ اللَّهُ (وَلاَ تُصَلِّ عَلَى أَحَدٍ مِنْهُمْ مَاتَ أَبَدًا وَلاَ تَقُمْ عَلَى قَبْرِهِ) فَتَرَكَ الصَّلاَةَ عَلَيْهِمْ.

Ibn 'Umar narrated that when 'Abdullah ibn Ubayy died, his son came to the Prophet (ﷺ) and said, "O Messenger of Allah, give me your shirt to shroud him, lead his funeral prayer and ask forgiveness for him." So Allah's Messenger (ﷺ) gave him his shirt and said, "*Inform me (when the prayer is ready) and I will lead the prayer for him.*" When he informed him and the Prophet (ﷺ) was about to lead the funeral prayer, 'Umar took hold of his hand and asked, "Hasn't Allah forbidden you from praying for the hypocrites?" He replied, "*I have two choices: Either to ask for their forgiveness or not ask for their forgiveness.*"[16] So he led the funeral prayer and the verse: ﴿Do not ever pray for any of them who die...﴾ was revealed.[17] So he (ﷺ) stopped praying for them.

'Abdullah ibn 'Umar reported that, after that Allah's Messenger (ﷺ) never prayed for a *munāfiq* (hypocrite) nor stood by his grave until Allah took him.[18]

عَنْ سَعِيد بْنِ الْمُسَيَّبِ عَنْ أَبِيهِ قَالَ: لَمَّا حَضَرَتْ أَبَا طَالِبٍ الْوَفَاةُ دَخَلَ عَلَيْهِ النَّبِيُّ ﷺ وَعِنْدَهُ أَبُو جَهْلٍ وَعَبْدُاللَّهِ بْنُ أَبِي أُمَيَّةَ فَقَالَ النَّبِيُّ

[16] This is in reference to verse 80 of chapter *at-Tawbah* (9).

[17] Bukhari (Arabic-English), vol. 2, Pp. 201-2 hadith no. 359, Muslim (English trans), vol. 4, Pp. 1456-7, hadith no. 6680, and *Sunan Ibn Mājah*, vol. 2, p. 401, hadith no. 1523.

[18] See Muslim (English trans), vol. 4, Pp. 1457, hadith no. 6681.

ﷺ : أَيْ عَمِّ قُلْ لاَ إِلَهَ إِلاَّ اللَّهُ أُحَاجُّ لَكَ بِهَا عِنْدَ اللَّهِ فَقَالَ أَبُو جَهْلٍ وَعَبْدُاللَّهِ بْنُ أَبِي أُمَيَّةَ يَا أَبَا طَالِبٍ أَتَرْغَبُ عَنْ مِلَّةِ عَبْدِالْمُطَّلِبِ فَقَالَ النَّبِيُّ ﷺ : ((لأَسْتَغْفِرَنَّ لَكَ مَا لَمْ أُنْهَ عَنْكَ)) فَنَزَلَتْ ﴿ مَا كَانَ لِلنَّبِيِّ وَالَّذِينَ آمَنُوا أَنْ يَسْتَغْفِرُوا لِلْمُشْرِكِينَ وَلَوْ كَانُوا أُولِي قُرْبَى مِنْ بَعْدِ مَا تَبَيَّنَ لَهُمْ أَنَّهُمْ أَصْحَابُ الْجَحِيمِ ﴾

Al-Musayyib ibn Ḥazn reported that when (the Prophet's uncle), Abu Ṭālib, was on his deathbed, the Prophet (ﷺ) went to see him. Abu Jahl and 'Abdullah ibn Abi Umayyah were also there with him. He said, "*O uncle, say, "There is no god worthy of worship but Allah, so that I may plead your case with it before Allah.*" On hearing that, Abu Jahl and 'Abdullah ibn Abi Umayyah said, "O Abu Ṭālib, will you renounce the religion of (our father) 'Abdul-Muṭṭalib?" The Prophet (ﷺ) then said, "*I will continue to ask forgiveness for you as long as I am not prohibited.*" Then Allah revealed the verse: ﴿The Prophet and Believers should not seek forgiveness for the idolaters even if they were near relatives, once it is made clear that they are inhabitants of the Hell-Fire.﴾ (Qur'an 9: 113)."[19]

B. The *Jamā'ah* (Congregation)

1) In congregation

Ṣalātul-Janāzah, like the five daily compulsory prayers, must be performed in congregation. This was the only way that the Prophet (ﷺ) and his Companions did it. The Prophet (ﷺ) is also reported to have said,

---

[19] Bukhari (Arabic-English), vol. 6, p. 158, hadith no. 197 and *Ṣaḥīḥ Muslim*, vol. 1, p. 18, hadith no. 36.

((وَصَلُّوا كَمَا رَأَيْتُمُونِي أُصَلِّي))

"Pray as you saw me pray."[20]

The only exception to this rule was in the case of the funeral prayer for the Prophet (ﷺ) in which the Prophet's Companions all prayed separately due to the uniqueness of the situation and their state of confusion at the time.[21]

2) Three Rows

It is preferable that those behind the Imām form at least three rows, as this was the *Sunnah* when the number of worshippers was insufficient to fill the masjid. Abu Umāmah reported that the Prophet (ﷺ) led the *ṣalāh* for the dead along with seven people and he made them form three rows, two of which had two people in them.[22] Mālik ibn Hubayrah also reported that the Prophet (ﷺ) said,

((مَا مِنْ مُسْلِمٍ يَمُوتُ فَيُصَلِّي عَلَيْهِ ثَلَاثَةُ صُفُوفٍ مِنَ الْمُسْلِمِينَ إِلاَّ أَوْجَبَ)).

"Any Muslim who dies and three rows of Muslims make ṣalāh for him, will be forgiven."[23]

---

[20] Bukhari (Arabic-English), vol. 1, p. 345, hadith no. 604.

[21] *Al-Bidāyah wa an-Nihāyah*, vol. 5, Pp. 304-5.

[22] *Aḥkām al-Janā'iz*, p. 99 with support of the following hadith.

[23] *Sunan Abi Dāwūd*, vol. 2, p. 899, hadith no. 3160 and *Mishkāt al-Maṣābīḥ*, vol. 1, Pp. 353-4. This is an authentic saying of the *Ṣaḥābi* and not the Prophet's saying. See *Ḍa'īf Sunan Abi Dāwūd*, Pp. 320-1, hadith no. 695 and *Ḍa'īf Ibn Mājah*, p. 113 hadith no. 327. Also see *Aḥkām al-Janā'iz*, p. 100.

3) Two Men

If there is only one man besides the Imām, he should pray behind the Imām and not beside him as in the case of all other *ṣalāhs*.

عَنْ عبدِ اللهِ بِنْ أَبِي طَلْحَةَ أَنَّ طَلْحَةَ دَعَا رَسُولَ اللَّهِ ﷺ إِلَى عُمَيْرِ بْنِ أَبِي طَلْحَةَ حِينَ تُوُفِّيَ، فَأَتَاهُ رَسُولُ اللَّهِ ﷺ فَصَلَّى عَلَيْهِ فِي مَنْزِلِهِمْ، فَتَقَدَّمَ رَسُولُ اللَّهِ ﷺ، وَ كَانَ أَبُو طَلْحَةَ وَرَاءَهُ وَ أُمُّ سُلَيْمٍ وراءَ أَبِي طَلْحَةَ، وَ لَمْ يَكُنْ مَعَهُمْ غَيْرُهُمْ.

'Abdullah ibn Abi Ṭalḥah reported that Abu Ṭalḥah called for Allah's Messenger (ﷺ) when 'Umayr ibn Abi Ṭalḥah died. The Messenger of Allah (ﷺ) came and made *ṣalāh* for him in their house. Allah's Messenger (ﷺ) stepped forward and Abu Ṭalḥah stood behind him, and Umm Sulaym stood behind Abu Ṭalḥah. There was no one else there with them.[24]

4) The Imām

The *Amīr* or his assistant has more right to lead the funeral prayer than the deceased's *wali*, nearest male relative. Abu Ḥāzim said, "Verily, I was present on the day of al-Ḥasan ibn 'Ali's death and I heard al-Ḥusayn ibn 'Ali say to Sa'īd ibn al-'Āṣ,[25] "Go forward (and lead the *ṣalāh*), for if it was not (in accordance with the) *Sunnah*, I wouldn't have put you forward." He said that because there was some ill feeling between them.[26]

---

[24] Collected by al-Bayhaqi, al-Ḥākim, and aṭ-Ṭabarānī and authenticated in *Aḥkām al-Janā'iz*, p. 100.

[25] Sa'īd ibn al-'Āṣ was the *Amīr* of al-Madīnah at that time. He was a *Ṣaḥābi* and one of those who wrote out copies of the 'Uthmāni Qur'an.

[26] Collected by al-Bayhaqi and authenticated in *Aḥkām al-Janā'iz*, Pp.100-01.

If neither the *Amīr* nor his representative is present, the one who has memorized the most Qur'an should lead the funeral prayer, even if he is a child.

عَنْ عَمْرِو بْنِ سَلَمَةَ عَنْ أَبِيهِ أَنَّهُمْ وَفَدُوا إِلَى النَّبِيِّ ﷺ فَلَمَّا أَرَادُوا أَنْ يَنْصَرِفُوا قَالُوا يَا رَسُولَ اللَّهِ مَنْ يَؤُمُّنَا قَالَ: ((أَكْثَرُكُمْ جَمْعًا لِلْقُرْآنِ أَوْ أَخْذًا لِلْقُرْآنِ)) قَالَ فَلَمْ يَكُنْ أَحَدٌ مِنَ الْقَوْمِ جَمَعَ مَا جَمَعْتُهُ قَالَ فَقَدَّمُونِي وَأَنَا غُلامٌ وَعَلَيَّ شَمْلَةٌ لِي فَمَا شَهِدْتُ مَجْمَعًا مِنْ جَرْمٍ إِلاَّ كُنْتُ إِمَامَهُمْ وَكُنْتُ أُصَلِّي عَلَى جَنَائِزِهِمْ إِلَى يَوْمِي هَذَا.

'Amr ibn Salamah reported that when a delegation from his tribe, which had come to the Prophet (ﷺ), prepared to leave, they asked, "O Messenger of Allah, who should lead us in *ṣalāh*?" He replied, "*The one who has memorized the most Qur'an.*" Since none of the tribe had memorized more than me, they put me forward — even though I was only a youth (of six or seven at the time).[27] Whenever I was present at a gathering, I was made the Imām and I have lead the *ṣalāḥ* on their dead until this day."[28]

5) A Number of Dead

If there are a number of dead people, a single *ṣalātul-janāzah* can be made for all of them. However, if there are males and females, the female bodies are placed in front of the Imām and the males behind the Imām even if they are young children. Nāfi' reported that Ibn 'Umar led the funeral prayer for nine dead Muslims with

[27] This addition is found in Bukhari (Arabic-English), vol. 5, Pp. 413-4, hadith no. 595.

[28] *Sunan Abi Dāwūd*, vol. 1, p. 155, hadith no. 587 and authenticated by Shaykh al-Albāni in *Ṣaḥīḥ Sunan Abi Dāwūd*, vol. 1, p. 117, hadith no. 548.

the dead males behind him and the dead females in front of him in one row.[29]

عَنْ عَمَّارٌ مَوْلَى الْحَارِثِ بْنِ نَوْفَلٍ أَنَّهُ شَهِدَ جَنَازَةَ أُمِّ كُلْثُوم وَابْنِهَا فَجُعِلَ الْغُلَامُ مِمَّا يَلِي الإِمَامَ فَأَنْكَرْتُ ذَلِكَ وَفِي الْقَوْمِ ابْنُ عَبَّاسٍ وَأَبُو سَعِيدٍ الْخُدْرِيُّ وَأَبُو قَتَادَةَ وَأَبُو هُرَيْرَةَ فَقَالُوا: هَذِهِ السُّنَّةُ.

'Ammār, the freed slave of al-Ḥārith ibn Nawfal related that he attended the funeral prayer of Umm Kulthūm[30] and her son (Zayd) and the (body of the) youth was placed behind the Imām. He disputed it. Ibn 'Abbās, Abu Sa'īd al-Khudri, Abu Qatādah and Abu Hurayrah were among the people and they said, "This is the Sunnah."[31]

It is also allowable that *Ṣalātul-Janāzah* be performed on each person individually as this was also done on occasion by the Prophet (ﷺ). A prayer for each is the basic practice.

عَنِ ابْنِ عَبَّاسٍ قَالَ: لَمَّا وَقَفَ رَسُولُ اللَّهِ عَلَى حَمْزَةَ .. أَمَرَ بِهِ فَهُيِّئَ إِلَى الْقِبْلَةِ، ثُمَّ كَبَّرَ عَلَيْهِ تِسْعًا، ثُمَّ جُمِعَ إِلَيْهِ الشُّهَدَاءُ، كُلَّمَا أُتِيَ بِشَهِيدٍ وُضِعَ إِلَى حَمْزَةَ فَصَلَّى عَلَيْهِ وَعَلَى الشُّهَدَاءِ مَعَهُ حَتَّى صَلَّى عَلَيْهِ وَعَلَى الشُّهَدَاءِ اثْنَيْنِ وَسَبْعِينَ صَلاَةً.

Ibn 'Abbās said, "When Allah's Messenger came across Ḥamzah, he asked for him and his body was prepared and placed in the direction of Makkah. He then prayed the funeral prayer using nine *takbīrs*. Then the bodies of the other martyrs were brought. Each

---

[29] Collected by an-Nasā'i (1:280), al-Bayhaqi (4:33) and ad-Dāraquṭni (194), and authenticated in *Aḥkām al-Janā'iz*, p. 103.

[30] The daughter of 'Ali ibn Abi Ṭālib and the wife of 'Umar ibn al-Khaṭṭāb.

[31] *Sunan Abi Dāwūd*, vol. 2, p. 906, hadith no. 3187 and authenticated by Shaykh al-Albāni in *Ṣaḥīḥ Sunan Abi Dāwūd*, vol. 2, Pp. 614-5, hadith no. 2734.

martyr's body was placed beside Ḥamzah's body, one at a time, and he prayed for each along with Ḥamzah's body until he completed seventy-two funeral prayers.[32]"

C. Location of the Prayer

1) Inside the masjid

The common practice today of holding the funeral prayer inside the masjid is based on the occasional practice of the Prophet (ﷺ).

عَنْ عَبَّادِ بْنِ عَبْدِ اللَّهِ بْنِ الزُّبَيْرِ أَنَّ عَائِشَةَ أَمَرَتْ أَنْ يَمُرَّ بِجَنَازَةِ سَعْدِ بْنِ أَبِي وَقَّاصٍ فِي الْمَسْجِدِ فَتُصَلِّيَ عَلَيْهِ فَأَنْكَرَ النَّاسُ ذَلِكَ عَلَيْهَا فَقَالَتْ مَا أَسْرَعَ مَا نَسِيَ النَّاسُ مَا صَلَّى رَسُولُ اللَّهِ ﷺ عَلَى سُهَيْلِ بْنِ الْبَيْضَاءِ إِلاَّ فِي الْمَسْجِدِ.

'Abbād, the son of 'Abdillah ibn az-Zubayr, related that 'Ā'ishah (and the Prophet's wives)[33] requested that the bier of Sa'd ibn Abi Waqqāṣ be brought to the masjid so that she could also pray for him. (Those carrying the bier brought it and placed it in front of their apartments[34] and they offered prayer for him).[35] When the people heard about it, they began to criticize her [and say that it was *bid'ah* (innovation) and that the bier should not be taken into the masjid. When 'Ā'ishah heard that,][36] she said, "How quickly people have forgotten that Allah's Messenger (ﷺ) prayed for

[32] Collected by aṭ-Ṭabarānī in *Al-Kabīr*, vol. 3, Pp. 107-8 and authenticated in *Aḥkām al-Janā'iz*, Pp. 104-5.

[33] This addition is in Muslim (English trans), vol. 2, Pp. 460-1, hadith no. 2124.

[34] The doors of the apartments of the Prophet's wives opened into the masjid.

[35] This addition is in Muslim (English trans), vol. 2, Pp. 460-1, hadith no. 2124.

[36] This addition is in Muslim (English trans), vol. 2, Pp. 460-1, hadith no. 2124.

Suhayl ibn Bayḍā (and his brother)[37] inside the masjid."[38]

2) Outside the Masjid

It is however preferable to have a place (*muṣallā*) set aside for the funeral prayer outside the masjid, as this was the usual practice of the Prophet (ﷺ).

عَنْ أَبِي هُرَيْرَةَ رَضِي اللَّهُ عَنْهُ قَالَ نَعَى لَنَا رَسُولُ اللَّهِ ﷺ النَّجَاشِيَّ صَاحِبَ الْحَبَشَةِ يَوْمَ الَّذِي مَاتَ فِيهِ فَقَالَ: ((اسْتَغْفِرُوا لِأَخِيكُمْ)) وَ صَفَّ بِهِمْ بِالْمُصَلَّى فَكَبَّرَ عَلَيْهِ أَرْبَعًا.

Abu Hurayrah reported that when Allah's Messenger (ﷺ) announced the death of the ruler (*najāshi*) of Ethiopia to them on the day that he died, he said, "*Ask forgiveness for your brother,*" and had them line up in rows at the *muṣallā* and prayed for him using four *takbīrs*.[39]

عَنْ عَبْدِاللَّهِ بْنِ عُمَرَ رَضِي اللَّهُ عَنْهُمَا أَنَّ الْيَهُودَ جَاءُوا إِلَى النَّبِيِّ ﷺ بِرَجُلٍ مِنْهُمْ وَامْرَأَةٍ زَنَيَا فَأَمَرَ بِهِمَا فَرُجِمَا قَرِيبًا مِنْ مَوْضِعِ الْجَنَائِزِ عِنْدَ الْمَسْجِدِ.

---

[37] Ibid., p. 461, hadith no. 2125.

[38] Reported by 'Ā'ishah and collected in Muslim (English trans), vol. 2, p. 460, hadith no. 2123. The final statement of 'Ā'ishah "How quickly... inside the masjid," can also be found in *Sunan Abi Dāwūd*, vol. 2, p. 905, hadith no. 3183, *Sunan Ibn Mājah*, vol. 2, p. 404, hadith no. 1518, *Muwaṭṭa*, Pp. 108-9, hadith no. 534 and *Mishkāt al-Maṣābīḥ*, vol. 1, p. 348.

[39] Bukhari (Arabic-English), vol. 2, p. 191, hadith no. 337, Muslim (English trans), vol. 2, p. 452, hadith no. 2077, *Sunan Abi Dāwūd*, vol. 2, p. 911, hadith no. 3198, *Sunan Ibn Mājah*, vol. 2, p. 412, hadith no. 1534, *Mishkāt al-Maṣābīḥ*, vol. 1, p. 348 and *Muwaṭṭa*, p. 107, hadith no. 526.

'Abdullah ibn 'Umar also reported that the Jews came to the Prophet (ﷺ) with a man and woman who had committed adultery, so he ordered that they be stoned near the place for funeral (prayers) beside the masjid."[40]

3) Between the Graves

It is forbidden for *Ṣalātul-Janāzah* to be said for the dead between the graves according to the following hadith narrated by Anas ibn Mālik in which he said,

((أَنَّ النَّبِيَّ ﷺ نَهَى أَن يُّصَلِّيَ عَلَى الْجَنَائِزِ بَيْنَ الْقُبُورِ))

"The Prophet (ﷺ) forbade the performance of the *ṣalāh* for the dead in between the graves."[41]

D. The Method of Prayer

1) Position of the Imām

The Imām should stand, facing the Qiblah, behind the head of the dead man and behind the middle of the dead woman,

عَنْ نَافِعٍ أَبِي غَالِبٍ قَالَ كُنْتُ فِي سِكَّةِ الْمِرْبَدِ فَمَرَّتْ جَنَازَةٌ مَعَهَا نَاسٌ كَثِيرٌ قَالُوا جَنَازَةُ عَبْدِ اللَّهِ بْنِ عُمَيْرٍ فَتَبِعْتُهَا فَإِذَا أَنَا بِرَجُلٍ عَلَيْهِ كِسَاءٌ رَقِيقٌ عَلَى بُرَيْذِينَتِهِ وَعَلَى رَأْسِهِ خِرْقَةٌ تَقِيهِ مِنَ الشَّمْسِ فَقُلْتُ مَنْ هَذَا الدِّهْقَانُ قَالُوا هَذَا أَنَسُ بْنُ مَالِكٍ فَلَمَّا وُضِعَتِ الْجَنَازَةُ قَامَ أَنَسٌ فَصَلَّى عَلَيْهَا وَأَنَا خَلْفَهُ لاَ يَحُولُ بَيْنِي وَبَيْنَهُ شَيْءٌ فَقَامَ عِنْدَ رَأْسِهِ فَكَبَّرَ أَرْبَعَ

---

[40] Bukhari (Arabic-English), vol. 2, Pp. 231-2, hadith no. 413.

[41] Collected by aṭ-Ṭabarānī and authenticated in *Aḥkām al-Janā'iz*, p. 108, hadith no. 72.

تَكْبِيرَاتٍ لَمْ يُطِلْ وَلَمْ يُسْرِعْ ثُمَّ ذَهَبَ يَقْعُدُ فَقَالُوا يَا أَبَا حَمْزَةَ الْمَرْأَةُ الْأَنْصَارِيَّةُ فَقَرَّبُوهَا وَعَلَيْهَا نَعْشٌ أَخْضَرُ فَقَامَ عِنْدَ عَجِيزَتِهَا فَصَلَّى عَلَيْهَا نَحْوَ صَلَاتِهِ عَلَى الرَّجُلِ ثُمَّ جَلَسَ فَقَالَ الْعَلَاءُ بْنُ زِيَادٍ: يَا أَبَا حَمْزَةَ هَكَذَا كَانَ يَفْعَلُ رَسُولُ اللَّهِ ﷺ يُصَلِّي عَلَى الْجَنَازَةِ كَصَلَاتِكَ يُكَبِّرُ عَلَيْهَا أَرْبَعًا وَيَقُومُ عِنْدَ رَأْسِ الرَّجُلِ وَعَجِيزَةِ الْمَرْأَةِ قَالَ: نَعَمْ.

Nāfi‘ Abu Ghālib said, "While I was in *Sikkatul-Mirbad,*[42] a bier passed by with a large number of people accompanying it. They informed me that it was the bier of ‘Abdullah ibn ‘Umayr, so I followed it. I noticed (among them) a man wearing a thin cloak riding on a mule. He had a piece of cloth on his head to protect himself from the sun. I asked who this important man was and they replied that it was Anas ibn Mālik. When the bier was set down, Anas stood up and led the funeral prayer for him. I was standing immediately behind him with nothing between him and me. He stood near the deceased's head and made four *takbīrs.* He neither lengthened the prayer nor made it hastily. When he went to sit down, they said to him, "O Abu Ḥamzah, (here is the bier of) an Anṣari woman. They brought her near to him and there was a green coloured *na‘sh*[43] over her. He stood opposite her hip[44] and led the funeral prayer in the same way as he done for the dead

---

[42] *Sikkah* literally means 'a wide street' or 'an even road' in which the houses are in rows on either side, and *mirbad* literally means 'an enclosure for camels, sheep or goats' or 'a place in which dates are put to dry after cutting' (*Arabic-English Lexicon*, vol. 1, Pp. 1010 & 1386). *Sikkatul-Mirbad* was the name of a subdivision in Baṣrah.

[43] An arched canopy put as a cover over a dead woman when she is placed on a bier. (*Arabic-English Lexicon*, vol. 2, p. 2816) This was done to maintain her privacy in death as in life.

[44] Literally *‘ajīzah* means buttocks, backside, posterior.

man. He then sat down. Al-'Alā ibn Ziyād[45] asked, "O Abu Ḥamzah, did Allah's Messenger (ﷺ) make the funeral prayer for the dead as you did, using four *takbīrs* and standing opposite the head of a man and the hips of a woman?" He replied, "Yes."[46]

2) Number of *Takbirs*

It is possible to do either four, five, six, seven or nine *takbīrs* as all of them are recorded in authentic hadiths and acts of the Prophet's Companions.

Four:

عَنْ أَبِي هُرَيْرَةَ رَضِي اللَّهُ عَنْهُ أَنَّ رَسُولَ اللَّهِ ﷺ نَعَى النَّجَاشِيَّ فِي الْيَوْمِ الَّذِي مَاتَ فِيهِ وَخَرَجَ بِهِمْ إِلَى الْمُصَلَّى فَصَفَّ بِهِمْ وَكَبَّرَ عَلَيْهِ أَرْبَعَ تَكْبِيرَاتٍ.

Abu Hurayrah related that the Messenger of Allah (ﷺ) announced the Najāshi's death on the same day which he died and went out with them to a place designated for large congregational prayers. He arranged them in rows and pronounced **four** *takbīrs* during the funeral prayer.[47]

---

[45] He was among the most reliable narrators of hadith among the *Tābi'ūn* from Baṣrah. However, among the six major hadith collections, his hadiths were cited only by an-Nasā'i and Ibn Mājah. He died in 94 AH.

[46] *Sunan Abi Dāwūd*, vol. 2, Pp. 907-8, hadith no. 3188, *Sunan Ibn Mājah*, vol. 2, Pp. 391-2, hadith no. 1494 and *Mishkāt al-Maṣābīḥ*, vol. 1, p. 352 and authenticated by Shaykh al-Albāni in *Ṣaḥīḥ Sunan Abi Dāwūd*, vol. 2, p. 615, hadith no. 2735.

[47] Bukhari (Arabic-English), vol. 2, p. 227, hadith no. 404, Muslim (English trans), vol. 2, p. 452, hadith no. 2077, *Sunan Abi Dāwūd*, vol. 2, p. 911, hadith no. 3198, *Sunan Ibn Mājah*, vol. 2, p. 412, hadith no. 1534, *Mishkāt al-Maṣābīḥ*, vol. 1, p. 348, and *Muwaṭṭa*, p. 107, hadith no. 526.

Five:

عَنِ ابْنِ أَبِي لَيْلَى قَالَ كَانَ زَيْدٌ يَعْنِي ابْنَ أَرْقَمَ يُكَبِّرُ عَلَى جَنَائِزِنَا أَرْبَعًا وَإِنَّهُ كَبَّرَ عَلَى جَنَازَةٍ خَمْسًا فَسَأَلْتُهُ فَقَالَ كَانَ رَسُولُ اللَّهِ ﷺ يُكَبِّرُهَا.

'Abdur-Raḥmān ibn Abi Laylā said, "Zayd ibn Arqam used to make **four** *takbīrs* on our dead, but once he made **five** so we asked him about it. He replied, 'Allah's Messenger used to do it and I would not give it up for anyone after him, ever.'"[48]

Six:

عَنْ عَبْدُ خَيْرٍ قَالَ: كَانَ عَلِيٌّ رَضِيَ اللَّهُ عَنْهُ يُكَبِّرُ عَلَى أَهْلِ بَدْرٍ سِتًّا، وَ عَلَى أَصْحَابِ النَّبِيِّ ﷺ خَمْسًا، وَعَلَى سَائِرِ النَّاسِ أَرْبَعًا.

'Abd Khayr said, "Ali ibn Abi Ṭālib used to make **six** *takbīrs* (when he led funeral prayers) on those who took part in the Battle of Badr, **five** *takbīrs* on the Prophet's Companions, and **four** *takbīrs* on all the rest of the people."[49]

Seven:

عَنْ مُوسَى بْنِ عَبْدِ اللَّهِ بْنِ يَزِيدٍ أَنَّ عَلِيًّا صَلَّى عَلَى قَتَادَةَ فَكَبَّرَ عَلَيْهِ سَبْعًا، وَكَانَ بَدْرِيًّا.

Mūsā, the son of 'Abdullah ibn Yazīd, said that 'Ali ibn Abi Ṭālib made the funeral prayer using **seven** *takbīrs* for Abu Qatādah,

---

[48] Muslim (English trans), vol. 2, Pp. 453-4, hadith no. 2089, *Sunan Abi Dāwūd*, vol. 2, Pp. 908-9, hadith no. 3191, *Sunan Ibn Mājah*, vol. 2, p. 397, hadith no. 1505 and *Mishkāt al-Maṣābīḥ*, vol. 1, p. 348.

[49] Collected by al-Bayhaqi and ad-Dāraquṭni and authenticated in *Aḥkām al-Janā'iz*, p. 113.

who was among those who took part in the Battle of Badr.[50]

Nine:

عَنْ عَبْدِ اللَّهِ بْنِ الزُّبَيْرِ أَنَّ النَّبِيَّ صَلَّى عَلَى حَمْزَةَ فَكَبَّرَ عَلَيْهِ تِسْعَ تَكْبِيرَاتٍ.

'Abdullah ibn az-Zubayr reported that the Prophet (ﷺ) made the funeral prayer for Ḥamzah using **nine** *takbīrs*.[51]

3) Raising the Hands

It is permissible to either raise one's hands with each *takbīr,* or to do so only for the first *takbīr.*

عَنْ ابْنِ عَبَّاسٍ أَنَّ رَسُولَ اللَّهِ ﷺ كَانَ يَرْفَعُ يَدَيْهِ عَلَى الْجَنَازَةِ فِي أَوَّلِ تَكْبِيرَةٍ، ثُمَّ لاَ يَعُودُ.

Ibn 'Abbās reported that Allah's Messenger (ﷺ) used to raise his hands for the **first** *takbīr* in the funeral prayer, then not repeat it.[52]

It is also reported that Ibn 'Umar used to raise his hands with every *takbīr* of the funeral prayer.[53]

4) Placing the hands

The right hand should be placed on the left on the chest as in regular prayer since there are no authentic hadiths to indicate

---

[50] Collected by al-Bayhaqi and authenticated in *Aḥkām al-Janā'iz*, Pp. 113-4.

[51] Collected by aṭ-Ṭaḥāwī and aṭ-Ṭabarānī and authenticated in *Aḥkām al-Janā'iz*, p. 114.

[52] Collected by ad-Dāraquṭni and authenticated in *Aḥkām al-Janā'iz*, p. 116.

[53] Collected by al-Bayhaqi (4:44) and authenticated in *Aḥkām al-Janā'iz*, p. 117. See also Bukhari (Arabic-English), vol. 2, p. 228, Chapter 55.

otherwise.

عَنْ سَهْلِ بْنِ سَعْدٍ قَالَ: كَانَ النَّاسُ يُؤْمَرُونَ أَنْ يَضَعَ الرَّجُلُ الْيَدَ الْيُمْنَى عَلَى ذِرَاعِهِ الْيُسْرَى فِي الصَّلاَةِ قَالَ أَبُو حَازِمٍ لاَ أَعْلَمُهُ إِلاَّ يَنْمِي ذَلِكَ إِلَى النَّبِيِّ صَلَّى اللَّهُ عَلَيْهِ وَسَلَّمَ.

The Prophet's Companion, Sahl ibn Sa'd said, "The people were ordered to place their right hands on their left forearms in *ṣalāh*."[54] Ṭāwūs[55] also said, "Allah's Messenger (ﷺ) used to place his right hand on his left and tighten them on his chest when in *ṣalāh*."[56]

5) Recitation

Immediately after the first *takbīr*, the chapter *al-Fātiḥah* should be read as this is what is recorded in authentic hadiths.

عَنْ طَلْحَةَ بْنِ عَبْدِ اللَّهِ بْنِ عَوْفٍ قَالَ: صَلَّيْتُ خَلْفَ ابْنِ عَبَّاسٍ عَلَى جَنَازَةٍ فَقَرَأَ بِفَاتِحَةِ الْكِتَابِ، قَالَ: لِتَعْلَمُوا أَنَّهَا سُنَّةٌ.

Ṭalḥah, the son of 'Abdullah ibn 'Awf, said, "I prayed the funeral prayer behind Ibn 'Abbās for a dead person and he recited (aloud) the *Fātiḥah* and said, "Know that (what I have done) is the Sunnah."[57]

---

54 Bukhari (Arabic-English), vol. 1, Pp. 396-7, hadith no. 707 and *Mishkāt al-Maṣābīḥ*, vol. 1, p. 161.

55 Ṭāwūs ibn Kīsān was among the middle level students of the Companions of the Prophet.

56 *Sunan Abu Dāwūd*, vol. 1, p. 194, hadith no. 758; and authenticated by Shaykh al-Albāni in *Ṣaḥīḥ Sunan Abi Dāwūd*, vol. 1, p. 144, hadith no. 687.

57 Bukhari (Arabic-English), vol. 2, p. 236, hadith no. 419 and *Sunan Abi Dāwūd*, vol. 2, p. 909, hadith no. 3192.

The only thing which should be read prior to the *Fātiḥah* is the "Refuge" and the "*basmalah*".[58]

أَعُوذُ بِاللَّهِ مِنَ الشَّيْطَانِ الرَّجِيمِ مِنْ نَفْخِهِ وَنَفْثِهِ وَهَمْزِهِ

A'ūdhu bil-lāhi minash-shayṭānir-rajīmi min nafakhihi wa nafathihi wa hamzih (I seek refuge in Allah from the accursed *Shayṭān*, from his pride, his poetry, and his madness).[59]

There are no hadiths, neither authentic nor weak, to support the reading of the *Du'ā al-Istiftāḥ* (the opening *du'ā*: *subḥānakal-lāhumma*).

It is also permissible to recite another chapter after reciting *Fātiḥah.* This is based on another narration of Ṭalḥah's statement in which he said,

((صَلَّيْتُ خَلْفَ ابْنِ عَبَّاسٍ عَلَى جِنَازَةٍ فَقَرَأَ بِفَاتِحَةِ الْكِتَابِ وَسُورَةٍ وَجَهَرَ حَتَّى أَسْمَعَنَا فَلَمَّا فَرَغَ أَخَذْتُ بِيَدِهِ فَسَأَلْتُهُ فَقَالَ سُنَّةٌ وَحَقٌّ)).

"I prayed the funeral prayer behind Ibn 'Abbās and he recited *Fātiḥah al-Kitāb* and another chapter loudly enough that we heard it. So when he finished, I took hold of his hand and asked him about it. He replied, "I said it loudly in order that you all would know that it was *Sunnah* and correct."[60]

---

[58] Bukhari (Arabic-English), vol. 1, p. 397, hadith no. 710, Muslim (English trans), vol. 1, p. 219, hadith no. 786 and *Muwaṭṭa*, p. 36 hadith no. 173.

[59] *Sunan Abi Dāwūd*, vol. 1, p. 196, hadith no. 763, *Sunan Ibn Mājah*, vol. 2, p. 4, hadith no. 808 and *Mishkāt al-Maṣābīḥ*, vol. 1, Pp. 166-167 and authenticated by Shaykh al-Albāni in *Ṣaḥīḥ Sunan Ibn Mājah*, vol. 1, Pp. 135-6, hadith no. 658.

[60] Bukhari (Arabic-English), vol. 2, p. 234 hadith no. 419, *Sunan Abi Dāwūd*, vol. 2, p. 909, hadith no. 3192, *Sunan Ibn Mājah*, vol. 2, p. 392, hadith no. 1495 and *Mishkāt al-Maṣābīḥ*, vol. 1, p. 348.

The recitation should be done quietly based on Abu Umāmah ibn Sahl's statement:

((السُّنَّةُ فِي الصَّلاَةِ عَلَى الْجَنَازَةِ أَنْ يَقْرَأَ فِي التَّكْبِيرَةِ الأُولَى بِأُمِّ الْقُرْآنِ مُخَافَتَةً ثُمَّ يُكَبِّرَ ثَلاَثًا وَالتَّسْلِيمُ عِنْدَ الآخِرَةِ)).

"The Sunnah in *Ṣalātul-Janāzah* is to quietly recite *Umm al-Qur'an*[61] after the first *takbīr*, then to make three *takbīrs* and *taslīm* at the end (of the prayer)."[62]

6) Prayer for the Prophet

Immediately after the second *takbīr*, the prayer for the Prophet (ﷺ) should be made according to one of the various patterns used in regular *ṣalāh*. In describing the funeral prayer Abu Umāmah went on to say, "Then the prayer for the Prophet (ﷺ) should be made."[63]

اللَّهُمَّ صَلِّ عَلَى مُحَمَّدٍ وَعَلَى آلِ مُحَمَّدٍ كَمَا صَلَّيْتَ عَلَى إِبْرَاهِيمَ إِنَّكَ حَمِيدٌ مَجِيدٌ اللَّهُمَّ بَارِكْ عَلَى مُحَمَّدٍ وَعَلَى آلِ مُحَمَّدٍ كَمَا بَارَكْتَ عَلَى آلِ إِبْرَاهِيمَ إِنَّكَ حَمِيدٌ مَجِيدٌ.

"*Allahumma ṣalli 'alā Muhammadin wa 'alā āli Muhammad,* (Oh Allah, praise Muhammad and his family) *kamā ṣallayta 'alā Ibrāhīma wa 'alā āli Ibrāhīm,* (as you have praised Ibrāhīm and his family.) *innaka ḥamīdun-majīd*. (Verily you are the Most Praised and Glorious). *Allahumma bārik 'alā Muhammadin wa 'alā āli Muhammad*, (O Allah, bless Muhammad and his family) *kamā bārakta 'alā Ibrāhīma wa 'alā āli Ibrāhīm* (as you have

[61] *Umm al-Qur'an* is among the names of the first chapter.

[62] *Ṣaḥīḥ Sunan an-Nasā'i* vol. 2, p. 428, hadith no. 1880.

[63] Ibid., and ash-Shāfi'i in *al-Umm* (1/239-240). See *Aḥkām al-Janā'iz*, p. 122.

blessed Ibrāhīm and his family). *innaka ḥamīdun majīd* (Verily, you are the Most Praised and Glorious).[64]

7) *Du'ā* for the Dead

After each of the remaining two or more *takbīrs*, sincere prayers should be made for the dead, their relatives and the living. Nothing from the Qur'an should be recited following these remaining *takbīrs*. The Prophet (ﷺ) is quoted as saying,

((إِذَا صَلَّيْتُمْ عَلَى الْمَيِّتِ فَأَخْلِصُوا لَهُ الدُّعَا)).

> *"When you make funeral prayers for the dead, make sincere du'ā for them."*[65]

The following are some authentic *du'ās* any one of which could be said after the third and fourth *takbīrs*:

١- اللَّهُمَّ اغْفِرْ لَهُ وَارْحَمْهُ وَعَافِهِ وَاعْفُ عَنْهُ وَأَكْرِمْ نُزُلَهُ وَوَسِّعْ مُدْخَلَهُ وَاغْسِلْهُ بِالْمَاءِ وَالثَّلْجِ وَالْبَرَدِ وَنَقِّهِ مِنَ الْخَطَايَا كَمَا يُنَقَّى الثَّوْبَ الأَبْيَض مِنَ الدَّنَسِ وَأَبْدِلْهُ دَارًا خَيْرًا مِنْ دَارِهِ وَأَهْلاً خَيْرًا مِنْ أَهْلِهِ وَزَوْجًا خَيْرًا مِنْ زَوْجِهِ وَأَدْخِلْهُ الْجَنَّةَ وَأَعِذْهُ مِنْ عَذَابِ الْقَبْرِ أَوْ مِنْ عَذَابِ النَّارِ

1. *Allahum-maghfir lahu war ḥamhu 'āfihi wa'fu 'anhu wa akrim nuzulahu wa wassi' madkhalah,* [Oh Allah, forgive him, have

---

[64] Bukhari (Arabic-English), vol. 4, p. 385, hadith no. 589, Muslim (English trans), vol. 1, p. 224, hadith no. 807, *Sunan Abi Dāwūd*, vol. 1, p. 249, hadith no. 971, *Sunan Ibn Mājah*, vol. 2, Pp. 54-5, hadith no. 904 and *Mishkāt al-Maṣābīḥ*, vol. 1, p. 188.

[65] *Sunan Abi Dāwūd*, vol. 2, p. 909, hadith no. 3193, *Sunan Ibn Mājah*, vol. 2, p. 393, hadith no. 1497, *Mishkāt al-Maṣābīḥ*, vol. 1, p. 351 and authenticated by Shaykh al-Albāni in *Ṣaḥīḥ Sunan Abi Dāwūd*, vol. 2, Pp. 616-7, hadith no. 2740.

mercy on him, make him well, overlook his faults, make his place of rest a noble place and expand (the door of) his entrance (into Paradise)] *waghsil-hu bil-mā wath-thalji wal-baradi wa naqqihu minal-khaṭāyā kamā yunnaqath-thawbul-abyaḍu minad-danas* (wash him with water, snow, and hail, and purify him of his sins the way a white cloth is purified of dirt) *wa abdilhu dāran khayran min dārih wa ahlah khayran min ablih wa zawjan khayran min zawjih* (replace his home with a better home, his family with a better family and his wife with a better spouse;) *wa ad-khilhul-jan-nah wa a'īdhu min 'adhābil-qabr wa min 'adhābin-nār.* (put him in Paradise and give him refuge from the punishment of the grave and the fire.)[66]

٢ـ اللَّهُمَّ اغْفِرْ لِحَيِّنَا وَمَيِّتِنَا وَصَغِيرِنَا وَكَبِيرِنَا وَذَكَرِنَا وَأُنْثَانَا وَشَاهِدِنَا وَغَائِبِنَا اللَّهُمَّ مَنْ أَحْيَيْتَهُ مِنَّا فَأَحْيِهِ عَلَى الإِيمَانِ وَمَنْ تَوَفَّيْتَهُ مِنَّا فَتَوَفَّهُ عَلَى الإِسْلَامِ اللَّهُمَّ لاَ تَحْرِمْنَا أَجْرَهُ وَلاَ تُضِلَّنَا بَعْدَهُ.

2. *Allahummaghfir liḥayyinā wa mayyitinā wa ṣaghīrinā wa kabīrinā wa dhakarinā wa unthānā wa shāhidinā wa ghā'ibinā.* (Oh Allah, forgive our living and our dead, our young ones and our elder ones, our males and our females, those of us who are present and those of us who are absent.) *Allahumma man aḥ-yaytahu min-nā fa aḥ-yihi 'alal-Eemān wa man tawaffayatahu min-nā fa tawaffahu 'alal-Islam.* [Oh Allah, whoever from among us that you keep living, keep him living in *Eemān* (faith) and whoever among us that you cause to die, take his life in a state of Islam.] *Allahumma lā taḥ-rimnā ajrahu wa lā tuḍillanā ba'dah*

[66] Reported by Abu Hurayrah in Muslim (English trans), vol. 2, Pp. 456-7, hadith nos. 2104 & 2106, *Sunan Ibn Mājah*, vol. 2, Pp. 394-5, hadith no. 1500 and *Mishkāt al-Maṣābīḥ*, vol. 1, p. 348.

(Oh Allah, do not deprive us of his reward and do not misguide us after him.)[67]

٣ـ ((أَللّهُمَّ عَبْدُكَ وَابْنُ أُمَّتِكَ إِحْتَاجَ إِلَى رَحْمَتِكَ وَأَنْتَ غَنِيٌّ عَنْ عَذَابِهِ، إِنْ كَانَ مُحْسِنًا فَزِدْهُ فِي حَسَنَاتِهِ وَ إِنْ كَانَ مُسِيْئًا فَتَجَاوَزْ عَنْهُ))

3. *Allahumma 'abduka wabnu ummatik iḥtāja ilā raḥmatik wa anta ghanīyun 'an 'adhābih* (Oh Allah, a slave of yours and a son of your nation needs your mercy and you have no need for his punishment.) *in kāna muḥsinan fazid-hu fi ḥasanātih* (If he was good, increase his good deeds) *wa in kāna musī'an fatajāwaz 'anh* (and if he was bad, overlook it.)[68]

8) *Taslīm*[69]

There are two ways in which the closing greetings of the funeral prayer may be given:

a) Either by saying: *As-salāmu 'alaykum wa raḥmatullah* (May

---

[67] Reported by Abu Hurayrah in *Sunan Abi Dāwūd*, vol. 2, Pp. 909-10, hadith no. 3195, *Sunan Ibn Mājah*, vol. 2, p. 393, hadith no. 1498 and *Mishkāt al-Maṣābīḥ*, vol. 1, Pp. 351-2 and authenticated by Shaykh al-Albāni in *Ṣaḥīḥ Sunan Abi Dāwūd*, vol. 2, p. 617, hadith no. 2741. Also collected by Tirmidhi and Aḥmad. Of the nine isnāds by which the hadith is reported in the major books, eight report it by the working: *Allahumma man aḥ-yaytahū min-nā fa aḥ-yihi 'alal-Islam wa man tawaffayatuhū min-nā fa tawaffahū 'alal-eemān.* [O Allah, whoever from among us that you keep living, keep him living in Islam and whoever among us thatyou cause to die, take his life in a state of *eemān* (faith)].

[68] Reported by Yazīd ibn Rukānah and collected by al-Ḥākim and Mālik (*Muwaṭṭa*, Pp. 107-8, hadith no. 529) and authenticated in *Aḥkām al-Janā'iz*, p. 125.

[69] The act of completing the formal prayer by giving greetings of *salām* (peace) is known as *taslīm*.

Allah's peace and mercy be upon you) to the right side only, as in Abu Hurayrah's hadith:

((أَنَّ رَسُولَ اللَّهِ ﷺ صَلَّى عَلَى جَنَازَةٍ فَكَبَّرَ عَلَيْهَا أَرْبَعًا، وَسَلَّمَ تَسْلِيمَةً وَاحِدَةً))

"Allah's Messenger made the funeral prayer by doing four *takbīrs* and one *taslīm*."[70]

b) Or by saying, "*As-salāmu 'alaykum wa raḥmatullāh*" to both sides, as in Ibn Mas'ūd's hadith:

((ثَلَاثٌ خِلَالٍ كَانَ رَسُولُ اللَّهِ ﷺ يَفْعَلُهُنَّ تَرَكَهُنَّ النَّاسُ، إِحْدَاهُنَّ التَّسْلِيمُ عَلَى الْجَنَازَةِ مِثْلَ التَّسْلِيمِ فِي الصَّلَاةِ))

"There are three things which Allah's Messenger (ﷺ) used to do and which people have neglected, one of them is making *taslīm* in the funeral prayer like the *taslīm* in (regular) *ṣalāh*..."[71]

9) Forbidden Times

There are three times in the day when *Ṣalātul-Janāzah* or any other *ṣalāh* is strictly forbidden except in the case of an emergency. These are the times during which the sun worshippers used (and use) to perform their rites of worship. Thus, these became forbidden times in order to avoid any resemblance to them and to prevent non-Muslims from thinking that Muslims might also be worshipping the sun.

---

[70] Collected by al-Bayhaqi, ad-Dāraquṭni and al-Ḥākim and authenticated in *Aḥkām al-Janā'iz*, p. 128, hadith no. 85.

[71] Collected by al-Bayhaqi and aṭ-Ṭabarānī and authenticated in *Aḥkām al-Janā'iz*, p. 127, hadith no. 83.

عَنْ عُقْبَةَ بْنِ عَامِرٍ الْجُهَنِيِّ قَالَ: ثَلاَثُ سَاعَاتٍ كَانَ رَسُولُ اللَّهِ ﷺ يَنْهَانَا أَنْ نُصَلِّيَ فِيهِنَّ أَوْ أَنْ نَقْبُرَ فِيهِنَّ مَوْتَانَا: حِينَ تَطْلُعُ الشَّمْسُ بَازِغَةً حَتَّى تَرْتَفِعَ، وَحِينَ يَقُومُ قَائِمُ الظَّهِيرَةِ حَتَّى تَمِيلَ الشَّمْسُ، وَحِينَ تَضَيَّفُ الشَّمْسُ لِلْغُرُوبِ حَتَّى تَغْرُبَ.

'Uqbah ibn 'Āmir said, "There are three times in which the Messenger of Allah (ﷺ) used to forbid us from making *ṣalāh* or burying our dead:

1) When the sun is rising until it (the disc of the sun) is clearly above the horizon.
2) When the sun reaches the middle of the sky until it declines.
3) When the sun is setting until it (completely) disappears.[72]"

[72] Muslim (English trans), vol. 2, p. 395, hadith no. 1811 & p. 906 hadith no. 3186, *Sunan Ibn Mājah*, vol. 2, p. 405, hadith no. 1519 and *Mishkāt al-Maṣābīḥ*, vol. 1, p. 213.

CHAPTER 5: THE BURIAL

A) Injunctions Regarding Burial

1) Burying Everyone

Muslims are obliged to bury everyone who dies in areas under their jurisdiction.

عَنْ عَلِيٍّ قَالَ: قُلْتُ لِلنَّبِيِّ ﷺ إِنَّ عَمَّكَ الشَّيْخَ الضَّالَّ قَدْ مَاتَ، قَالَ: ((اِذْهَبْ فَوَارِ أَبَاكَ، ثُمَّ لاَ تُحَدِّثَنَّ شَيْئًا حَتَّى تَأْتِيَنِي)) فَذَهَبْتُ فَوَارَيْتُهُ، وَجِئْتُهُ فَأَمَرَنِي فَاغْتَسَلْتُ وَدَعَا لِي.

'Ali said, "I told the Prophet (ﷺ), "Verily, your old misguided uncle has died." He said, "*Go and bury your father, then don't say anything until you come back to me.*" So I went and buried him and returned to the Prophet (ﷺ). He then instructed me to take a bath, which I did, and he prayed for me.[1]

2) Muslims Buried Separately

Muslims should not be buried beside non-Muslims, nor non-Muslims beside Muslims. Each should have their own separate graveyard.

---

[1] *Sunan Abi Dāwūd*, vol. 2, p. 914, hadith no. 3208 and authenticated by Shaykh al-Albāni in *Ṣaḥīḥ Sunan Abi Dāwūd*, vol. 2, p. 619, hadith no. 2753.

عَنْ بَشِيرٍ مَوْلَى رَسُولِ اللَّهِ ﷺ قَالَ: بَيْنَمَا أَنَا أُمَاشِي رَسُولَ اللَّهِ ﷺ، مَرَّ بِقُبُورِ الْمُشْرِكِينَ فَقَالَ: ((لَقَدْ سَبَقَ هَؤُلَاءِ خَيْرًا كَثِيرًا)) ثَلَاثًا. ثُمَّ مَرَّ بِقُبُورِ الْمُسْلِمِينَ فَقَالَ: ((لَقَدْ أَدْرَكَ هَؤُلَاءِ خَيْرًا كَثِيرًا)).

Bashīr,[2] the freed slave of Allah's Messenger, (ﷺ) said, "While I was walking with the Messenger of Allah (ﷺ), he passed by the graves of the pagans and said three times, "*They preceded a time of abundant good.*" Then he passed by the graves of the Muslims and said, "*They got abundant good.*"[3]

3) Burial in the Graveyard

It was the Prophet's *Sunnah* to bury the dead in the graveyard of Madīnah, known as *al-Baqi'*.

عَنْ عَائِشَةَ قَالَتْ رَجَعَ رَسُولُ اللَّهِ ﷺ مِنَ الْبَقِيعِ فَوَجَدَنِي وَأَنَا أَجِدُ صُدَاعًا فِي رَأْسِي وَأَنَا أَقُولُ وَا رَأْسَاهُ فَقَالَ: ((بَلْ أَنَا يَا عَائِشَةُ وَا رَأْسَاهُ)).

'Ā'ishah reported that when the Prophet (ﷺ) returned from a funeral at al-Baqi', she was suffering from a headache and said, "Oh, my head." The Prophet (ﷺ) replied, *"No, it is I who is in pain from whatever hurts you."*[4]

It was also the unanimous practice of the earlier generations of righteous Muslim scholars and their students.

---

[2] The narrator explained that his pre-Islamic name was Zaḥm ibn Ma'bad and that the Prophet renamed him 'Bashīr'.

[3] *Sunan Abi Dāwūd*, vol. 2, Pp. 917-8, hadith no. 3224 and authenticated by Shaykh al-Albāni in *Ṣaḥīḥ Sunan Abi Dāwūd*, vol. 2, p. 622, hadith no. 2767.

[4] *Sunan Ibn Mājah*, vol. 2, p. 376, hadith no. 1465 and *Mishkāt al-Maṣābīḥ*, vol. 2, p. 1308 and authenticated by Shaykh al-Albāni in *Ṣaḥīḥ Sunan Ibn Mājah*, vol. 1, p. 247, hadith no. 1197.

The burial of the Prophet (ﷺ) in his home was an exception based on his own indirect instructions.

عَنْ عَائِشَةَ قَالَتْ: لَمَّا قُبِضَ رَسُولُ اللَّهِ ﷺ اِخْتَلَفُوا فِي دَفْنِهِ، فَقَالَ أَبُو بَكْرٍ: سَمِعْتُ مِنْ رَسُولِ اللَّهِ ﷺ شَيْئًا مَا نَسِيْتُهُ قَالَ: ((مَا قَبَضَ اللَّهُ نَبِيًا إِلاَّ فِي الْمَوْضِعِ الَّذِي يُحِبُّ أَنْ يُدْفَنَ فِيْهِ)) فَدَفَنُوهُ فِي مَوْضِعِ فِرَاشِهِ.

'Ā'ishah said, "When Allah's Messenger (ﷺ) died, they differed concerning his burial. Abu Bakr said, "I heard the Messenger of Allah (ﷺ) say, "*Allah only takes a prophet in the place where he likes to be buried.*" So they buried him where his bed was."[5]

4) Depth of the Grave

The grave should be dug deep and wide, and be well prepared.

عَنْ هِشَامِ بْنِ عَامِرٍ قَالَ: قَالَ رَسُولُ اللَّهِ ﷺ: ((اِحْفِرُوا وَأَوْسِعُوا وَأَحْسِنُوا)).

Hishām ibn 'Āmir reported that Allah's Messenger (ﷺ) said, "*Dig the grave deep, make it spacious and prepare it well.*"[6]

5) Shape of the Grave

The grave may be dug straight down (*shaqq*) with a burial chamber in the middle or with a niche (*laḥd*) to create the burial chamber on the side. However, in both cases a burial chamber is

---

[5] *Sunan Ibn Mājah*, vol. 2, Pp. 467-70, hadith no. 1627 and authenticated by Shaykh al-Albāni in *Ṣaḥīḥ Sunan at-Tirmidhi*, vol. 1, p. 298, hadith no. 812.

[6] *Sunan Ibn Mājah*, vol. 2, p. 425, hadith no. 1560 and authenticated by Shaykh al-Albāni in *Ṣaḥīḥ Sunan Ibn Mājah*, vol. 1, p. 260, hadith no. 1266.

created from the earth, and sealed with bricks of unbaked clay.[7] Both methods were in practice in the time of the Prophet (ﷺ).

عَنْ أَنَسِ بْنِ مَالِكٍ قَالَ لَمَّا تُوُفِّيَ النَّبِيُّ صَلَّى اللَّهُ عَلَيْهِ وَسَلَّمَ كَانَ بِالْمَدِينَةِ رَجُلٌ يَلْحَدُ وَآخَرُ يَضْرَحُ فَقَالُوا نَسْتَخِيرُ رَبَّنَا وَنَبْعَثُ إِلَيْهِمَا فَأَيُّهُمَا سُبِقَ تَرَكْنَاهُ فَأُرْسِلَ إِلَيْهِمَا فَسَبَقَ صَاحِبُ اللَّحْدِ فَلَحَدُوا لِلنَّبِيِّ .

Anas ibn Mālik said, "When the Prophet (ﷺ) died, there was a man in Madīnah who used to prepare a niched-grave and another who used to dig a straight-grave." They said, "We asked our Lord for the best, and sent for both of them on the basis that whoever came last would not be chosen. The one who made niched-graves came first, so they made a niched-grave for the Prophet (ﷺ)."[8]

However, the Prophet (ﷺ) favoured the *laḥd* style.

عَنِ ابْنِ عَبَّاسٍ قَالَ: قَالَ رَسُولُ اللَّهِ ﷺ : ((اللَّحْدُ لَنَا، وَالشَّقُ لِغَيْرِنَا)).

Ibn 'Abbās related that Allah's Messenger (ﷺ) said, "*The niched-grave is for us, and the straight-grave is for others.*"[9]

6) Number of Bodies in a Grave

Two or more bodies may be buried together in the same grave. This may be due to the large number of dead resulting from a

---

[7] See Muslim (English trans), vol. 2, Pp. 458-9, hadith no. 2112.

[8] *Sunan Ibn Mājah*, vol. 2, p. 423, hadith no. 1557 and authenticated by Shaykh al-Albāni in *Ṣaḥīḥ Sunan Ibn Mājah*, vol. 1, Pp. 259-60, hadith no. 1264.

[9] *Sunan Abi Dāwūd*, vol. 2, p. 912, hadith no. 3202 and *Sunan Ibn Mājah*, vol. 2, Pp. 421-2, hadith no. 1554 and authenticated by Shaykh al-Albāni in *Ṣaḥīḥ Sunan Ibn Mājah*, vol. 1, p. 259, hadith no. 1261.

natural calamity or plague, or the dead may be from the same family.

عَنْ جَابِرِ بْنِ عَبْدِ اللَّهِ أَنَّ رَسُولَ اللَّهِ ﷺ كَانَ يَجْمَعُ بَيْنَ الرَّجُلَيْنِ وَالثَّلاثَةِ مِنْ قَتْلَى أُحُدٍ فِي ثَوْبٍ وَاحِدٍ ثُمَّ يَقُولُ أَيُّهُمْ أَكْثَرُ أَخْذًا لِلْقُرْآنِ فَإِذَا أُشِيرَ لَهُ إِلَى أَحَدِهِمْ قَدَّمَهُ فِي اللَّحْدِ وَقَالَ : ((أَنَا شَهِيدٌ عَلَى هَؤُلاَءِ.)) وَأَمَرَ بِدَفْنِهِمْ فِي دِمَائِهِمْ وَلَمْ يُصَلِّ عَلَيْهِمْ وَلَمْ يُغَسَّلُوا.

Jābir ibn 'Abdillah related that Allah's Messenger (ﷺ) used to put two or three men who were killed during the battle of Uḥud in a single shroud and ask, "*Who among them knew the most Qur'an?*" When one was pointed out, he would be placed first in the grave. Then he would say, "*I am a witness for these men,*" and instruct that they be buried without removing the blood from their bodies. He also did not pray the funeral prayer for them nor wash them.[10]

B) Injunctions Concerning Placing the Body in the Grave:

1) Men

It is preferable that only men should be responsible for placing the dead body inside the grave, even if the dead person is a woman. This is due to the fact that it has been the custom among Muslims from the time of the Prophet (ﷺ) until today. The process requires a certain amount of strength and men are generally stronger than women. Furthermore, if women took on this responsibility, their

[10] Bukhari (Arabic-English), vol. 2, p. 239, hadith no. 427, *Sunan Ibn Mājah*, vol. 2, p. 403, hadith no. 1514 and *Sunan Abi Dāwūd*, vol. 2, p. 893, hadith no. 3132 and authenticated by Shaykh al-Albāni in *Ṣaḥīḥ Sunan Abi Dāwūd*, vol. 2, p. 606, hadith no. 2691.

effort to place the body in the grave would likely lead to the exposure of some parts of their bodies during the process.

2) Near Relatives

The blood relatives of the dead have more right to place the body in the grave based on the general meaning of the following Qur'anic verse:

﴿... وَأُوْلُواْ ٱلْأَرْحَامِ بَعْضُهُمْ أَوْلَىٰ بِبَعْضٍ فِي كِتَٰبِ ٱللَّهِ ...﴾ (٧٥)

(سورة الانفال ٨: ٧٥)

﴿...Blood relatives have more right to one another in Allah's scripture...﴾ (Qur'an 8: 75)

عَنِ عَبْدِ الرَّحْمَنِ بْنِ أَبْزَى قَالَ: صَلَّيْتُ مَعَ عُمَرَ بْنِ الْخَطَّابِ عَلَى زَيْنَبَ بِنْتِ جَحْشٍ بِالْمَدِينَةِ، فَكَبَّرَ أَرْبَعًا ثُمَّ أَرْسَلَ إِلَى أَزْوَاجِ النَّبِيِّ ﷺ: مَنْ يَأْمُرْنَ أَنْ يُدْخِلَهَا الْقَبْرَ؟ قَالَ: وَكَانَ يُعْجِبُهُ أَنْ يَكُونَ هُوَ الَّذِي يَلِي ذَلِكَ، فَأَرْسَلْنَ إِلَيْهِ: أُنْظُرْ مَنْ كَانَ يَرَاهَا فِي حَالِ حَيَاتِهَا فَلْيَكُنْ هُوَ الَّذِي يُدْخِلُهَا الْقَبْرَ، فَقَالَ عُمَرُ: صَدَقْتُنَّ)).

'Abdur-Raḥmān ibn Abzā said, "I prayed the funeral prayer for Zaynab bint Jaḥsh[11] in Madīnah along with 'Umar ibn al-Khaṭṭāb and he made four *takbīrs*. Then he sent a message to the wives of the Prophet (ﷺ) asking who they instructed to put her body in the grave. It would have pleased 'Umar to have been the one who would be responsible for that. But they sent back the reply, "Find the one who was permitted to see her while she was alive[12] and let

[11] One of the wives of the Prophet (ﷺ) who was also his cousin.

[12] The only males who were permitted to see the wives of the Prophet (ﷺ) were their immediate blood relatives (*maḥārim*).

him be the one to put her in her grave." 'Umar replied, "They spoke the truth."[13]

The Husband is permitted to place his wife's body in her grave on condition that he did not have sexual relations with his wife the previous night. The woman's father or any other male may do so, as large as they did not have sexual relations with their wives the previous night.

عَنْ أَنَسِ بْنِ مَالِكٍ رَضِي اللَّهُ عَنْهُ قَالَ شَهِدْنَا بِنْتَ رَسُولِ اللَّهِ ﷺ قَالَ وَرَسُولُ اللَّهِ ﷺ جَالِسٌ عَلَى الْقَبْرِ فَرَأَيْتُ عَيْنَيْهِ تَدْمَعَانِ فَقَالَ: ((هَلْ مِنْكُمْ رَجُلٌ لَمْ يُقَارِفِ اللَّيْلَةَ ؟)) فَقَالَ أَبُو طَلْحَةَ أَنَا قَالَ ((فَانْزِلْ فِي قَبْرِهَا)) فَنَزَلَ فِي قَبْرِهَا وَقَبَرَهَا.

Anas ibn Mālik said, "We were in the funeral procession of the Messenger of Allah's daughter, (Ruqayyah), and Allah's Messenger (ﷺ) was sitting near the grave and I saw his eyes full of tears. He said, "*Is there anyone among you who did not have sexual relations with his wife last night?*" Abu Ṭalḥah[14] replied that he had not, so Allah's Messenger (ﷺ) told him to get down in her grave and bury her, which he did.[15] (And 'Uthmān ibn 'Affān[16] did not enter her grave.)[17]"

---

[13] Collected by aṭ-Ṭaḥāwi and al-Bayhaqi (3/35) and authenticated in *Aḥkām al-Janā'iz*, p.148.

[14] Ṭalḥah was not a close blood relative of the Prophet or his daughter.

[15] Bukhari (Arabic-English), vol. 2, p. 238, hadith no. 426.

[16] Ruqayyah's husband.

[17] Collected in *Musnad Aḥmad*, vol. 3, p. 229 and authenticated in *Aḥkām al-Janā'iz*, p. 149.

3) Feet first

It is preferable that the body be placed in the niche feet first. This is the recorded way of the Prophet (ﷺ).

عَنْ أَبِي إِسْحَاقَ قَالَ: أَوْصَى الْحَارِثُ أَنْ يُصَلِّيَ عَلَيْهِ عَبْدُ اللَّهِ بْنُ يَزِيدٍ، فَصَلَّى عَلَيْهِ ثُمَّ أَدْخَلَهُ الْقَبْرَ مِنْ قِبَلِ رِجْلَيْ الْقَبْرِ وَقَالَ: هَذَا مِنَ السُّنَّةِ.

Abu Isḥāq said, "Al-Ḥārith left a will that 'Abdullah ibn Yazīd should lead his funeral prayer." So he led his prayer, then placed him in his grave feet first and said, "This is from the Sunnah."[18]

4) On the Right Side

It has been Muslim custom, from the time of the Prophet (ﷺ) until today, to place the dead body in the grave on its right side with the face of the dead person towards the qiblah (Makkah).[19]

5) *Du'ā* (Supplication)

At the time of inserting the body in the grave, those handling the procedure are recommended to make one of the following short prayers:

عَنِ ابْنِ عُمَرَ: أَنَّ النَّبِيَّ ﷺ كَانَ إِذَا وَضَعَ الْمَيِّتَ فِي الْقَبْرِ قَالَ: ((بِسْمِ اللَّهِ وَعَلَى سُنَّةِ رَسُولِ اللَّهِ)).

---

[18] *Sunan Abi Dāwūd*, vol. 2, p. 913, hadith no. 3205 and authenticated by Shaykh al-Albāni in *Ṣaḥīḥ Sunan Abi Dāwūd*, vol. 2, p. 619, hadith no. 2754.

[19] Quoted by Shaykh Nāṣir in *Aḥkām al-Janā'iz*, p. 151, from *al-Muḥallā* (5/173). There is a hadith with a weak isnād that says the ka'bah is "your qiblah in life and death." (*Sunan Abi Dāwūd*, vol. 2, Pp. 809-10, hadith no. 2869).

Ibn 'Umar said, "Whenever the Prophet (ﷺ) placed a dead person in his grave, he would say, '*In the name of Allah, and according to the way (sunnah) of the Messenger of Allah.*'"[20]

عَنِ ابْنِ عُمَرَ قَالَ: كَانَ النَّبِيُّ ﷺ إِذَا أَدْخَلَ الْمَيِّتَ الْقَبْرَ، قَالَ: ((بِسْمِ اللَّهِ وَعَلَى مِلَّةِ رَسُولِ اللَّهِ)).

Ibn 'Umar said, "Whenever the Prophet (ﷺ) placed a dead person in his grave, he would say, '*In the name of Allah, and according to the religion of the Messenger of Allah.*'"[21]

قَالَ هِشَامُ: ((بِسْمِ اللَّهِ وَفِي سَبِيلِ اللَّهِ وَعَلَى مِلَّةِ رَسُولِ اللَّهِ)).

Hishām said, "Whenever the Prophet (ﷺ) placed a dead person in his grave, he would say, '*In the name of Allah, in the path of Allah and according to the religion of the Messenger of Allah.*'"[22]

6) Throwing Dirt on the Grave

It is recommended for those near the grave to throw three double-handfuls of dirt into the grave after the burial chamber has been sealed.

عَنِ أَبِي هُرَيْرَةَ أَنَّ رَسُولَ اللَّهِ ﷺ صَلَّى عَلَى جَنَازَةٍ ثُمَّ أَتَى قَبْرَ الْمَيِّتِ فَحَثَى عَلَيْهِ مِنْ قِبَلِ رَأْسِهِ ثَلاثًا.

---

[20] *Sunan Ibn Mājah*, vol. 2, Pp. 419-20, hadith no. 1150 and *Sunan Abi Dāwūd*, vol. 2, p. 913, hadith no. 3207 and authenticated by Shaykh al-Albāni in *Ṣaḥīḥ Sunan Abi Dāwūd*, vol. 2, p. 619, hadith no. 2752.

[21] *Sunan Ibn Mājah*, vol. 2, Pp. 419-20, hadith no. 1150 and authenticated by Shaykh al-Albāni in *Ṣaḥīḥ Sunan Ibn Mājah*, vol. 1, p. 259, hadith no. 1260.

[22] *Sunan Ibn Mājah*, vol. 2, Pp. 419-20, hadith no. 1150 and authenticated by Shaykh al-Albāni in *Ṣaḥīḥ Sunan Ibn Mājah*, vol. 1, p. 259, hadith no. 1260.

Abu Hurayrah narrated that Allah's Messenger (ﷺ) lead funeral prayers then went to the dead man's grave and threw three handfuls of dirt in his grave opposite his head.[23]

C) After Burial

1) Raising the Grave

It is recommended that the earth of the grave be slightly raised, no more than a palm's width, so as to be higher than the surrounding ground. This is in order that it be easily distinguishable and not disrespected. In time the raised portion will naturally shrink as the earth settles.

عَنْ جَابِرٍ رَضِيَ اللَّهُ عَنْهُ: أَنَّ النَّبِيَّ ﷺ أُلْحِدَ لَهُ لَحْدٌ، وَنُصِبَ عَلَيْهِ اللَّبِنُ نَصْبًا، وَرُفِعَ قَبْرُهُ مِنَ ٱلأَرْضِ نَحْوًا مِنْ شِبْرٍ.

Jābir related that a *laḥd* was dug in the Prophet's grave and earthen bricks were placed over it, and (the earth of) his grave was raised above the ground by approximately a palm's width.[24]

It is also preferable that the raised portion be rounded.

عَنْ سُفْيَانَ التَّمَّارِ : رَأَيْتُ قَبْرَ النَّبِيِّ ﷺ وَقَبْرَ أَبِي بَكْرٍ وَعُمَرَ مُسَنَّمًا.

Sufyān at-Tammār said, "I saw the graves of the Prophet (ﷺ), Abu Bakr, and 'Umar and they were rounded."[25]

---

[23] *Sunan Ibn Mājah*, vol. 2, p. 427, hadith no. 1565 and authenticated by Shaykh al-Albāni in *Ṣaḥīḥ Sunan Ibn Mājah*, vol. 1, p. 261, hadith no. 1271.

[24] Collected by Ibn Ḥibbān (2160) and al-Bayhaqi (3/410) and authenticated in *Aḥkām al-Janā'iz*, p. 153.

[25] Bukhari (Arabic-English), vol. 2, p. 267, hadith no. 473. The addition of the graves of Abu Bakr and 'Umar is from Ibn Abi Shaybah's narration.

2) Marking the Grave

Placing a stone or something similar without inscriptions to identify the location of the grave is also from the *sunnah.* The marker will help people later locate the grave in order to bury other family members in the same vicinity.

عَنِ الْمُطَّلِبِ قَالَ لَمَّا مَاتَ عُثْمَانُ بْنُ مَظْعُونٍ أُخْرِجَ بِجَنَازَتِهِ فَدُفِنَ فَأَمَرَ النَّبِيُّ ﷺ رَجُلاً أَنْ يَأْتِيَهُ بِحَجَرٍ فَلَمْ يَسْتَطِعْ حَمْلَهُ فَقَامَ إِلَيْهَا رَسُولُ اللَّهِ ﷺ وَحَسَرَ عَنْ ذِرَاعَيْهِ [قَالَ كَثِيرٌ قَالَ الْمُطَّلِبُ قَالَ الَّذِي يُخْبِرُنِي ذَلِكَ عَنْ رَسُولِ اللَّهِ ﷺ قَالَ كَأَنِّي أَنْظُرُ إِلَى بَيَاضِ ذِرَاعَيْ رَسُولِ اللَّهِ ﷺ حِينَ حَسَرَ عَنْهُمَا] ثُمَّ حَمَلَهَا فَوَضَعَهَاعِنْدَ رَأْسِهِ وَقَالَ: ((أَتَعَلَّمُ بِهَا قَبْرَ أَخِي وَأَدْفِنُ إِلَيْهِ مَنْ مَاتَ مِنْ أَهْلِي)).

Al-Muṭṭalib[26] said, "When 'Uthmān ibn Ma<u>dh</u>'ūn died, he was carried out on his bier and buried." The Prophet (ﷺ) requested a man to bring him a rock, but he was unable to lift it. Therefore the Messenger of Allah (ﷺ) went to it and rolled up his sleeves.[27] He then carried the stone, placed it near the head of the grave and said,

> *"I am marking my brother's[28] grave with it, and I shall bury beside him those of my family who die."*[29]

---

[26] Al-Muṭṭalib ibn Abi Widā'ah was a well known Companion of the Prophet who accepted Islam at the time of the conquest of Makkah.

[27] Al-Muṭṭalib said, "The one who told me about Allah's Messenger (ﷺ) said, *'It is as though I can still see the whiteness of Allah's Messenger's forearms when he rolled up his sleeves.*'"

[28] 'Uthmān was the foster-brother of the Prophet.

[29] *Sunan Abi Dāwūd*, vol. 2, Pp. 912-3, hadith no. 3200 and authenticated by Shaykh al-Albāni in *Ṣaḥīḥ Sunan Abi Dāwūd*, vol. 2, p. 618, hadith no. 2745.

3) Structures Over Graves

The building of any kind of structures over graves is strictly prohibited.

عَنْ جَابِرٍ قَالَ نَهَى رَسُولُ اللَّهِ ﷺ أَنْ يُجَصَّصَ الْقَبْرُ وَأَنْ يُقْعَدَ عَلَيْهِ وَأَنْ يُبْنَى عَلَيْهِ.

Jābir related that Allah's Messenger (ﷺ) forbade the plastering of graves, or that they be sat upon, or that any structure be built over them[30] (or that anything be written on them)[31].

4) *Du'ā* (Supplication)

On the completion of the burial, it is recommended that those present at the grave-site offer prayers on behalf of the deceased:

عَنْ عُثْمَانَ بْنِ عَفَّانَ قَالَ كَانَ النَّبِيُّ ﷺ إِذَا فَرَغَ مِنْ دَفْنِ الْمَيِّتِ وَقَفَ عَلَيْهِ فَقَالَ: ((اسْتَغْفِرُوا لِأَخِيكُمْ وَسَلُوا لَهُ بِالتَّثْبِيتِ فَإِنَّهُ الْآنَ يُسْأَلُ)).

'Uthmān ibn 'Affān said, "Whenever the Prophet (ﷺ) finished burying a person, he would stand at the grave and say,

> *"Ask forgiveness for your brother, and pray for his steadfastness, for he is now being questioned."*"[32]

---

[30] Muslim (English trans), vol. 2, p. 459, hadith no. 2116 and *Sunan Abi Dāwūd*, vol. 2, p. 216, hadith no. 3219.

[31] *Sunan Abi Dāwūd*, vol. 2, Pp. 216-7, hadith no. 3220; and authenticated by Shaykh al-Albāni in *Ṣaḥīḥ Sunan Abi Dāwūd*, vol. 2, p. 621, hadith no. 2763.

[32] *Sunan Abi Dāwūd*, vol. 2, p. 915, hadith no. 3215 and authenticated by Shaykh al-Albāni in *Ṣaḥīḥ Sunan Abi Dāwūd*, vol. 2, p. 620, hadith no. 2758.

CHAPTER 6: BENEFITTING THE DEAD

The Qur'an established two general principles concerning the reward and punishment for deeds:

1) Each human will fundamentally only be benefitted or harmed by the deeds which he or she actually did.

﴿وَأَن لَّيْسَ لِلْإِنسَـٰنِ إِلَّا مَا سَعَىٰ ﴿٣٩﴾﴾ (سورة النجم ٥٣: ٣٩)

﴾That humans will only have the result of their actions.﴿ (Qur'an 53: 39)

2) No human can carry the sin of another.

﴿أَلَّا تَزِرُ وَازِرَةٌ وِزْرَ أُخْرَىٰ ﴿٣٨﴾﴾ (سورة النجم ٥٣: ٣٨)

﴾That no one bearing sins can carry the sins of others.﴿ (Qur'an 53: 38)

Consequently, when a person dies, the opportunity for that person to do good ends with the person's death. However, the chance to harvest good from deeds which were done prior to death remains.

1) *Du'ā*

The prayers of other Muslims on behalf of the dead will benefit the dead, by the permission of God. Had they done no good, no one would consider praying for them. If they were evil, the prayers of others will not benefit them. In chapter *al-Ḥashr* (59):10, Allah praises the believers who pray for those who have passed away before their time.

﴿وَٱلَّذِينَ جَآءُو مِنۢ بَعْدِهِمْ يَقُولُونَ رَبَّنَا ٱغْفِرْ لَنَا وَلِإِخْوَٰنِنَا ٱلَّذِينَ سَبَقُونَا بِٱلْإِيمَٰنِ وَلَا تَجْعَلْ فِى قُلُوبِنَا غِلًّا لِّلَّذِينَ ءَامَنُوا۟ رَبَّنَآ إِنَّكَ رَءُوفٌ رَّحِيمٌ ﴿١٠﴾﴾ (سورة الحشر ٥٩ : ١٠)

﴾And those who came after them say, "Our Lord, forgive us and our brothers who preceded us in faith, and do not put in our hearts any hatred against the believers. Our Lord, You are indeed full of kindness, Most Merciful."﴿ (Qur'an 59: 10)

Furthermore, the funeral prayer itself consists mostly of prayers for the dead.

عَنْ صَفْوَانَ وَهُوَ ابْنُ عَبْدِ اللَّهِ بْنِ صَفْوَانَ وَكَانَتْ تَحْتَهُ الدَّرْدَاءُ قَالَ قَدِمْتُ الشَّامَ فَأَتَيْتُ أَبَا الدَّرْدَاءِ فِي مَنْزِلِهِ فَلَمْ أَجِدْهُ وَوَجَدْتُ أُمَّ الدَّرْدَاءِ فَقَالَتْ أَتُرِيدُ الْحجَّ الْعَامَ فَقُلْتُ نَعمْ قَالَتْ فَادْعُ اللَّهَ لَنَا بِخَيْرٍ فَإِنَّ النَّبِيَّ ﷺ كَانَ يَقُولُ : ((دَعْوَةُ الْمَرْءِ الْمُسْلِمِ لأَخِيهِ بِظَهْرِ الْغَيْبِ مُسْتَجَابَةٌ عِنْدَ رَأْسِهِ مَلَكٌ مُوَكَّلٌ كُلَّمَا دَعَا لأَخِيهِ بِخَيْرٍ قَالَ الْمَلَكُ الْمُوَكَّلُ بِهِ آمِينَ وَلَكَ بِمِثْلٍ)) قَالَ فَخَرَجْتُ إِلَى السُّوقِ فَلَقِيتُ أَبَا الدَّرْدَاءِ فَقَالَ لِي مِثْلَ ذَلِكَ يَرْوِيهِ عَنِ النَّبِيِّ ﷺ.

Ṣafwān[1] said, "I visited Abu ad-Dardā's home in Syria, but did not find him there. Ummud-Dardā asked (me), "Are you going to make Ḥajj this year?" I said yes and she said, "Pray to Allah for good for us, for the Prophet (ﷺ) said, "*The prayer of a Muslim for his Muslim brother in his absence will be answered. As long as he prays for the good of his brother, there is an angel assigned near*

[1] The narrator mentioned, that is, Ṣafwān ibn 'Abdillah ibn Ṣafwān, had been (previously) married to Umm ad-Dardā.

his head who says: Amīn and may the same be for you." I left and went to the market place where I met Abu ad-Dardā and he related from the Prophet (ﷺ) the same as that."[2]

2) Fasting

Fasts missed by dead persons may be done on their behalf by their close relatives. The fasts may be from Ramaḍān or from oaths (*nadhar*).

عَنْ عَائِشَةَ رَضِي اللَّهُ عَنْهَا أَنَّ رَسُولَ اللَّهِ صَلَّى اللَّهُ عَلَيْهِ وَسَلَّمَ قَالَ : ((مَنْ مَاتَ وَعَلَيْهِ صِيَامٌ صَامَ عَنْهُ وَلِيُّهُ)).

'Ā'ishah quoted Allah's Messenger (ﷺ) as saying, "*Whoever died owing fasts, his guardian should fast on his behalf.*"[3]

عَنِ ابْنِ عَبَّاسٍ قَالَ : جَاءَ رَجُلٌ إِلَى النَّبِيِّ فَقَالَ : يَا رَسُولَ اللَّهِ إِنَّ أُمِّي مَاتَتْ وَعَلَيْهَا صَوْمُ شَهْرٍ أَفَأَقْضِيهِ عَنْهَا؟ قَالَ: ((نَعَمْ، فَدَيْنُ اللَّهِ أَحَقُّ أَنْ يُقْضَى)).

Ibn 'Abbās said, "A man came to the Prophet (ﷺ) and asked, "O Messenger of Allah, my mother died owing one month of fasting. Should I do it for her?" He replied, "*Yes, Allah's debts have more right to be paid.*"[4] In another narration a woman asked about her debt of fasting and got the same reply."

---

[2] Muslim (English trans), vol. 4, p. 1429, hadith no. 6590.

[3] Bukhari (Arabic-English), vol. 3, p. 99, hadith no. 173 and Muslim (English trans), vol. 2, p. 556, hadith no. 2553.

[4] Ibid, hadith no. 174 and Muslim (English trans), vol. 2, p. 556, hadith no. 2554.

3) Paying Financial Debts

Anyone may cover the debts of a dead person, whether they are relatives or not. Furthermore, the payment of outstanding debts can benefit the dead by relieving them from some of the punishment which was due to their negligence in repaying them.

عَنْ جَابِرٍ قَالَ تُوُفِّيَ رَجُلٌ فَغَسَّلْنَاهُ وَحَنَّطْنَاهُ وَكَفَّنَّاهُ ثُمَّ أَتَيْنَا بِهِ رَسُولَ اللَّهِ ﷺ يُصَلِّي عَلَيْهِ فَقُلْنَا تُصَلِّي عَلَيْهِ فَخَطَا خُطًى ثُمَّ قَالَ أَعَلَيْهِ دَيْنٌ قُلْنَا دِينَارَانِ فَانْصَرَفَ فَتَحَمَّلَهُمَا أَبُو قَتَادَةَ فَأَتَيْنَاهُ فَقَالَ أَبُو قَتَادَةَ الدِّينَارَانِ عَلَيَّ فَقَالَ رَسُولُ اللَّهِ ﷺ : ((أُحِقَّ الْغَرِيمُ وَبَرِئَ مِنْهُمَا الْمَيِّتُ)) قَالَ : نَعَمْ فَصَلَّى عَلَيْهِ ثُمَّ قَالَ بَعْدَ ذَلِكَ بِيَوْمٍ : ((مَا فَعَلَ الدِّينَارَانِ ؟)) فَقَالَ إِنَّمَا مَاتَ أَمْسِ قَالَ فَعَادَ إِلَيْهِ مِنَ الْغَدِ فَقَالَ لَقَدْ قَضَيْتُهُمَا فَقَالَ رَسُولُ اللَّهِ ﷺ ((اَلآنَ بَرَدَتْ عَلَيْهِ جِلْدُهُ)).

Jābir said, "A man died and we washed him, perfumed him and shrouded him. Then we brought him to Allah's Messenger (ﷺ) to lead the funeral prayer for him." We said, "Could you pray for him?" He took a step forward then asked, "*Does he have any outstanding debts?*" We answered, "Two dīnārs." (He said, "*Make the funeral prayer for your Companion,*" and)[5] he began to leave. Abu Qatādah took responsibility for (paying) them saying, "The two dīnārs are my responsibility." Allah's Messenger (ﷺ) said, "*Will the creditor get his rights and will the dead person be absolved from them?*" He replied, "Yes." So the Prophet (ﷺ) led the funeral prayer for him. One day later the Prophet (ﷺ) asked Abu Qatādah, "*What was done about the two dīnārs?*" He replied, "He only died yesterday!" The following day he returned to the Prophet (ﷺ) and said, "I have paid them

---

[5] This addition can be found in another narration of the hadith.

off." The Messenger of Allah (Blessings and Peace be upon him) said, "*Now his skin has become cool.*"[6]

4) The Charity of Children

Parents will benefit from whatever righteous deeds their children do, without decreasing the reward of their children's good deeds. A righteous child is considered to be part of the parent's earnings.

عَنْ عُمَارَةَ بْنِ عُمَيْرٍ عَنْ عَمَّتِهِ أَنَّهَا سَأَلَتْ عَائِشَةَ رَضِي اللَّهُ عَنْهَا فِي حِجْرِي يَتِيمٌ أَفَآكُلُ مِنْ مَالِهِ فَقَالَتْ قَالَ رَسُولُ اللَّهِ ﷺ ((إِنَّ مِنْ أَطْيَبِ مَا أَكَلَ الرَّجُلُ مِنْ كَسْبِهِ وَوَلَدُهُ مِنْ كَسْبِهِ)).

'Umārah ibn 'Umayr's aunt asked 'Ā'ishah, "I have an orphan under my guardianship. May I consume some of his wealth?" She replied that she had heard Allah's Messenger (Blessings and Peace be upon him) say,

> *"Among the most pleasant things a man consumes is what comes from his own earnings, and his child is from his earnings."*[7]

عَنْ عَائِشَةَ رَضِي اللَّهُ عَنْهَا أَنَّ رَجُلاً قَالَ لِلنَّبِيِّ ﷺ إِنَّ أُمِّي افْتُلِتَتْ نَفْسُهَا وَأَظُنُّهَا لَوْ تَكَلَّمَتْ تَصَدَّقَتْ فَهَلْ لَهَا أَجْرٌ إِنْ تَصَدَّقْتُ عَنْهَا قَالَ : ((نَعَمْ)).

'Ā'ishah related that a man asked the Prophet (ﷺ), "My mother died suddenly and I think that if she had spoken (before dying), she would have given something in charity. If I give charity on her

---

[6] *Musnad Aḥmad*, vol. 3, p. 330 and authenticated in *Aḥkām al-Janā'iz*, p. 16.

[7] *Sunan Abi Dāwūd*, vol. 2, p. 1002, hadith no. 3521 and authenticated by Shaykh al-Albāni in *Ṣaḥīḥ Sunan Abi Dāwūd*, vol. 2, p. 674, hadith no. 3013.

behalf, will she get the reward?" He replied: "Yes."[8]

عَنْ أَبِي هُرَيْرَةَ أَنَّ رَسُولَ اللَّهِ ﷺ قَالَ : ((إِذَا مَاتَ الْإِنْسَانُ انْقَطَعَ عَنْهُ عَمَلُهُ إِلاَّ مِنْ ثَلاَثَةٍ إِلاَّ مِنْ صَدَقَةٍ جَارِيَةٍ أَوْ عِلْمٍ يُنْتَفَعُ بِهِ أَوْ وَلَدٍ صَالِحٍ يَدْعُو لَهُ)).

Abu Hurayrah quoted the Messenger of Allah (ﷺ) as saying,

> *"When a man dies, his deeds come to an end, except in three cases: an on-going charity, knowledge from which people continue to benefit, and a righteous child who prays for him."*[9]

---

[8] Bukhari (Arabic-English), vol. 2, p. 266, hadith no. 470, Muslim (English trans), vol. 3, p. 866, hadith no. 4002 and *Sunan Abi Dāwūd*, vol. 2, p. 812, hadith no. 2875.

[9] Muslim (English trans), vol. 3, p. 867, hadith no. 4005 and *Sunan Abi Dāwūd*, vol. 2, p. 812, hadith no. 2874.

CHAPTER 7: VISITING GRAVES

Visiting graves is recommended in Islam in order to help the living reflect on the shortness of this life and the closeness of the next. In the Makkan period when Islam was first being spread, visiting graveyards was prohibited. Later on the Prophet permitted it.

عَنِ ابْنِ بُرَيْدَةَ عَنْ أَبِيهِ قَالَ قَالَ رَسُولُ اللَّهِ ﷺ : ((نَهَيْتُكُمْ عَنْ زِيَارَةِ الْقُبُورِ فَزُورُوهَا فَإِنَّ فِي زِيَارَتِهَا تَذْكِرَةً))

Buraydah related that Allah's Messenger (ﷺ) said,

> *"I forbade you from visiting graves, but now you may visit them, for in visiting them there is a reminder of death. (So whoever wishes to visit may do so, but don't say anything false)*[1]."[2]

Imām an-Nawawi stated that, "The prohibition was due to their closeness to the pre-Islamic period of ignorance, which could have led them to make inappropriate statements at the graves. When the foundations of Islam were firmly established, and its rules and principles had become well-known, visiting the graves was permitted. The Prophet (ﷺ) added, as a precaution, the warning, '*But don't say anything false.*'[3]

---

[1] This addition is found in an-Nasā'i's narration. See *Ṣaḥīḥ Sunan an-Nasā'i*, edited by Shaykh al-Albāni vol. 2, p. 436, hadith no. 1922.

[2] Muslim (English trans), vol. 2, p. 463, hadith no. 2131 and *Sunan Abi Dāwūd*, vol. 2, p. 919, hadith no. 3229. The wording quoted is that found in *Sunan Abi Dāwūd*.

[3] *Al-Majmū'*, vol. 3, p. 310.

1) Women Visiting Graves

The recommendation to visit graves is general and includes women, just as the earlier prohibition included them without any special mention. Furthermore, women share in the benefits of visiting the graves. In al-Ḥākim's narration from Anas ibn Mālik, the Prophet (ﷺ) is quoted as saying,

> *"Visit the (graves), because it softens the heart, brings tears to the eyes and reminds of the next life, but don't say anything false."*[4]

'Ā'ishah, wife of the Prophet (ﷺ) and one of the leading scholars among his followers, understood the permission to visit graves to include women.

عَنْ عَبْدِ اللَّهِ بْنِ أَبِي مُلَيْكَةَ أَنَّ عَائِشَةَ أَقْبَلَتْ ذَاتَ يَوْمٍ مِنَ الْمَقَابِرِ، فَقُلْتُ لَهَا: يَا أُمَّ الْمُؤْمِنِينَ مِنْ أَيْنَ أَقْبَلْتِ؟ قَالَتْ: مِنْ قَبْرِ عَبْدِ الرَّحْمَنِ بْنِ أَبِي بَكْرٍ، فَقُلْتُ لَهَا: أَلَيْسَ كَانَ رَسُولُ اللَّهِ ﷺ نَهَى عَنْ زِيَارَةِ الْقُبُورِ؟ قَالَتْ: نَعَمْ، ثُمَّ أَمَرَ بِزِيَارَتِهَا.

'Abdullah ibn Abi Mulaykah said, "One day when 'Ā'ishah came from the graveyard, I asked her, "O Mother of the Believers, where are you coming from?" She replied, "From 'Abdur-Raḥmān ibn Abi Bakr's grave." So I asked her, "Didn't Allah's Messenger (ﷺ) forbid the visiting of graves?" She replied, "Yes, then he instructed that they be visited."[5]

When the Prophet (ﷺ) found a woman crying in the graveyard, he did not chase her out of the graveyard, but told her not to cry.

---

[4] *Mustadrak al-Ḥākim*, vol. 1, p. 376 and authenticated in *Aḥkām al-Janā'iz*, p. 180.

[5] *Mustadrak al-Ḥākim*, vol. 1, p. 376 and *Sunan al-Bayhaqi*, vol. 4, p. 78 and authenticated in *Aḥkām al-Janā'iz*, p. 181.

عَنْ أَنَسِ بْنِ مَالِكٍ رَضِي اللَّهُ عَنْهُ قَالَ: مَرَّ النَّبِيُّ ﷺ بِامْرَأَةٍ تَبْكِي عِنْدَ قَبْرٍ فَقَالَ: ((اِتَّقِي اللَّهَ وَاصْبِرِي)).

Anas ibn Mālik related that once the Prophet (ﷺ) passed by a woman crying beside a grave and said to her, *"Fear Allah and be patient."*[6]

After mentioning this hadith under the heading 'Visiting Graves', Ibn Ḥajar said, "The (scholars) disagreed regarding women (visiting graves). The majority held that they are included in the general permission for visiting graves (if there is no danger of corruption). The ruling permitting women to visit graves is supported by the hadith of this chapter. The source of evidence in the hadith is the fact that he (ﷺ) did not censure the woman for sitting beside the grave and whatever he approves, is proof (of its permissibility)."[7]

However, frequent visitation of graves by women is not permissible.

عَنْ عَبْدِ الرَّحْمَنِ بْنِ حَسَّانِ بْنِ ثَابِتٍ عَنْ أَبِيهِ قَالَ لَعَنَ رَسُولُ اللَّهِ ﷺ زُوَّارَاتِ الْقُبُورِ.

Ḥassān ibn Thābit narrated that Allah's Messenger (ﷺ) cursed women who frequently visit graves.[8]

---

[6] Bukhari (Arabic-English), vol. 2, p. 208, hadith no. 372, Muslim (English trans), vol. 2, p. 439, hadith no. 2013, *Sunan Abi Dāwūd*, vol. 2, p. 890 hadith no. 3118, *Sunan Ibn Mājah*, vol. 2, p. 446 hadith no. 1596 and *Mishkāt al-Maṣābīḥ*, vol. 1, p. 361. The wording is from *Sunan Ibn Mājah*, vol. 2, p. 452, hadith no. 1605.

[7] *Fatḥ al-Bāri*, vol. 4, p. 244.

[8] *Sunan Ibn Mājah*, vol. 2, p. 433, hadith no. 1574 and authenticated by Shaykh al-Albāni in *Ṣaḥīḥ Sunan Ibn Mājah*, vol. 1, p. 263, hadith no. 1279.

Imām al-Qurṭubi said that the curse mentioned in the hadith is for those women who are frequent visitors as indicated by the intensive form of the word *zuwwārāt*[9]. Perhaps the reason for frequent visitation is the possible negative results of such visits like:

1) The loss of some of their husband's rights due to their frequent absences from the home,
2) The unnecessary public exposure of women,
3) Increased depression leading to wailing and other forbidden expressions of grief.[10]

2) Visiting Non-Muslim Graves

Although participation in the funeral rites of non-Muslims is not permitted, Muslims are allowed to visit the graves of disbelievers for reflection. However, praying for those who die in a state of disbelief is totally prohibited.

﴿ٱسْتَغْفِرْ لَهُمْ أَوْ لَا تَسْتَغْفِرْ لَهُمْ إِن تَسْتَغْفِرْ لَهُمْ سَبْعِينَ مَرَّةً فَلَن يَغْفِرَ ٱللَّهُ لَهُمْ﴾ (سورة التوبة ٩: ٨٠)

﴿Whether you ask forgiveness for them or you do not, even if you ask seventy times for their forgiveness, Allah will never forgive them.﴾ (Qur'an 9: 80)

﴿وَلَا تُصَلِّ عَلَىٰٓ أَحَدٍ مِّنْهُم مَّاتَ أَبَدًا وَلَا تَقُمْ عَلَىٰ قَبْرِهِۦٓ ...﴿٨٤﴾﴾

(سورة التوبة ٩: ٨٤)

---

[9] Some versions of the hadith use the word *zawwārāt*, which has the same meaning.

[10] Quoted in *Nayl al-Awtār*, vol. 4, Pp. 134-5.

﴾Do not make the funeral prayer for any of them who dies, nor stand at his grave.﴿ (Qur'an 9: 84)

Prophet Muhammad (ﷺ) was prevented by Allah from praying for his own mother, because she and his father had died as polytheists.

عَنْ أَبِي هُرَيْرَةَ قَالَ زَارَ النَّبِيُّ ﷺ قَبْرَ أُمِّهِ فَبَكَى وَأَبْكَى مَنْ حَوْلَهُ فَقَالَ ((اسْتَأْذَنْتُ رَبِّي فِي أَنْ أَسْتَغْفِرَ لَهَا فَلَمْ يُؤْذَنْ لِي وَاسْتَأْذَنْتُهُ فِي أَنْ أَزُورَ قَبْرَهَا فَأُذِنَ لِي فَزُورُوا الْقُبُورَ فَإِنَّهَا تُذَكِّرُ الْمَوْتَ)).

Abu Hurayrah related that the Prophet (ﷺ) visited the grave of his mother and cried and caused those around him to cry. Then he said,

> *"I asked my Lord's permission to pray for her forgiveness and permission was not granted to me. Then I asked His permission to visit her grave and he permitted me. So visit the graves, for it makes you mindful of death."*[11]

عَنْ أَنَسٍ أَنَّ رَجُلاً قَالَ يَا رَسُولَ اللَّهِ أَيْنَ أَبِي؟ قَالَ ((فِي النَّارِ)) فَلَمَّا قَفَّى دَعَاهُ فَقَالَ ((إِنَّ أَبِي وَأَبَاكَ فِي النَّارِ)).

Anas related that a man asked, "O Messenger of Allah, where is my father?" He replied, "*In the Hellfire.*" When he turned away, [the Prophet (ﷺ)] called him and said, "*Your father and my father are together in the Hellfire.*"[12]

In fact, Prophet Muhammad (ﷺ) instructed one of his Companions that whenever he passed by the grave of a disbeliever, he should

---

[11] Muslim (English trans), vol. 2, p. 463, hadith no. 2130, *Sunan Abi Dāwūd*, vol. 2, p. 919, hadith no. 3228 and *Sunan Ibn Mājah*, vol. 2, Pp. 431-2, hadith no. 1572.

[12] Muslim (English trans), vol. 1, p. 136, hadith no. 398.

announce for the disbeliever that his future abode will be the Hellfire.

عَنْ سَعْدِ بْنِ أَبِي وَقَّاصٍ قَالَ: جَاءَ أَعْرَابِيٌّ إِلَى النَّبِيِّ ﷺ فَقَالَ: إِنَّ أَبِي كَانَ يَصِلُ الرَّحِمَ، وَكَانَ وَكَانَ، فَأَيْنَ هُوَ؟ قَالَ: ((فِي النَّارِ)) فَكَأَنَّ الأَعْرَابِيَّ وَجَدَ مِنْ ذَلِكَ، فَقَالَ: يَا رَسُولَ اللَّهِ، فَأَيْنَ أَبُوكَ؟ قَالَ: ((حَيْثُمَا مَرَرْتَ بِقَبْرِ كَافِرٍ فَبَشِّرْهُ بِالنَّارِ)) قَالَ: فَأَسْلَمَ الأَعْرَابِيُّ بَعْدَ، فَقَالَ: لَقَدْ كَلَّفَنِي رَسُولُ للَّهِ ﷺ تَعْباً! مَا مَرَرْتُ بِقَبْرِ كَافِرٍ إِلاَّ بَشَّرْتُهُ بِالنَّارِ.

Sa'd ibn Abi Waqqāṣ reported that a Bedouin came to the Prophet (ﷺ) and asked, "My father used to maintain family ties, and he was this and that. So where is he?" He replied, "*In the Hellfire.*" It was as though the Bedouin found it difficult to handle, so he asked, "O Messenger of Allah, where is your father?" He replied, "*Whenever you pass by the grave of a disbeliever, announce to him his future in hell.*" The Bedouin accepted Islam after that and later said, "Allah's Messenger (ﷺ) burdened me with a tiresome responsibility. I haven't passed by the grave of a disbeliever without announcing to him that his future abode is hell."[13]

3) *Du'ā* (Supplication)

When visiting the graveyard, general prayers should be made for all of those buried there.

عَنْ مُحَمَّدِ بْنِ قَيْسِ بْنِ مَخْرَمَةَ بْنِ الْمُطَّلِبِ عَنْ عَائِشَةَ قَالَتْ قُلْتُ كَيْفَ أَقُولُ لَهُمْ يَا رَسُولَ اللَّهِ قَالَ: ((قُولِي السَّلَامُ عَلَى أَهْلِ الدِّيَارِ

[13] Collected by aṭ-Ṭabarānī in *al-Mu'jam al-Kabīr*, vol. 1, p. 191, hadith no. 1 and Ibn as-Sunni in *'Amal al-Yawm wal-Laylah*, hadith no. 588 and authenticated in *Aḥkām al-Janā'iz*, Pp. 198-9.

مِنَ الْمُؤْمِنِينَ وَالْمُسْلِمِينَ وَيَرْحَمُ اللَّهُ الْمُسْتَقْدِمِينَ مِنَّا وَالْمُسْتَأْخِرِينَ وَإِنَّا إِنْ شَاءَ اللَّهُ بِكُمْ لَلاحِقُونَ)).

Muhammad ibn Qays quoted 'Ā'ishah as saying, "I asked, "How should I pray for them, O Messenger of Allah?" He replied, "*Say: As-Salāmu 'alā ahlad-diyāri minal-mu'minīna wal-muslimīn* (Peace be on the believers and Muslim inhabitants of this city) *wa yarḥamullāh al-mustaqdimīna minnā wal-musta'khirīn* (May Allah have mercy on those who went before us and those coming after) *wa innā in shā Allahu bikum lalāḥiqūn* (Indeed, we shall — Allah willing — be joining you.)""""[14]

عَنْ سُلَيْمَانَ بْنِ بُرَيْدَةَ عَنْ أَبِيهِ قَالَ كَانَ رَسُولُ اللَّهِ ﷺ يُعَلِّمُهُمْ إِذَا خَرَجُوا إِلَى الْمَقَابِرِ فَكَانَ قَائِلُهُمْ يَقُولُ : السَّلاَمُ عَلَيْكُمْ أَهْلَ الدِّيَارِ مِنَ الْمُؤْمِنِينَ وَالْمُسْلِمِينَ وَإِنَّا إِنْ شَاءَ اللَّهُ لَلاحِقُونَ أَسْأَلُ اللَّهَ لَنَا وَلَكُمُ الْعَافِيَةَ.

Buraydah said, "Allah's Messenger (ﷺ) used to teach them what to say whenever they went out to the graveyard." They would say, "*As-Salāmu 'alaykum ahl ad-diyāri minal-mu'minīna wal-muslimīn* (Peace be on you, the believers and Muslim inhabitants of this city) *wa innā in shā Allahu lalāḥiqūn* (Indeed, we will — Allah willing — be joining you.) *as'alul-lāha lanā wa lakum al-'āfiyah* (I ask Allah for your well being and ours.)"[15]

4) Recitation of Qur'an

There is no basis for the recitation of Qur'an in the graveyard. Neither the *Fātiḥah* (First Chapter) nor any other chapter of the Qur'an should be read near the graves.

---

[14] Muslim (English trans), vol. 2, Pp. 461-2, hadith no. 2127.

[15] Ibid, hadith no. 2128.

عَنْ أَبِي هُرَيْرَةَ أَنَّ رَسُولَ اللَّهِ ﷺ قَالَ: ((لاَ تَجْعَلُوا بُيُوتَكُمْ مَقَابِرَ إِنَّ الشَّيْطَانَ يَنْفِرُ مِنَ الْبَيْتِ الَّذِي تُقْرَأُ فِيهِ سُورَةُ الْبَقَرَةِ)).

Abu Hurayrah reported that Allah's Messenger (Blessings and Peace be upon him) said,

> *"Don't make your houses graveyards, for surely Satan flees from the house in which the chapter al-Baqarah*[16] *is read."*[17]

5) Raising the Hands in *Du'ā*

The hands may be raised during supplications for the dead in the graveyard.

عَنْ عَائِشَةَ أَنَّهَا قَالَتْ خَرَجَ رَسُولُ اللَّهِ ﷺ ذَاتَ لَيْلَةٍ فَأَرْسَلْتُ بَرِيرَةَ فِي أَثَرِهِ لِتَنْظُرَ أَيْنَ ذَهَبَ قَالَتْ فَسَلَكَ نَحْوَ بَقِيعِ الْغَرْقَدِ فَوَقَفَ فِي أَدْنَى الْبَقِيعِ ثُمَّ رَفَعَ يَدَيْهِ ثُمَّ انْصَرَفَ فَرَجَعَتْ إِلَيَّ بَرِيرَةُ فَأَخْبَرَتْنِي فَلَمَّا أَصْبَحْتُ سَأَلْتُهُ فَقُلْتُ يَا رَسُولَ اللَّهِ أَيْنَ خَرَجْتَ اللَّيْلَةَ قَالَ: ((بُعِثْتُ إِلَى أَهْلِ الْبَقِيعِ لِأُصَلِّيَ عَلَيْهِمْ)).

'Ā'ishah said, "One night, Allah's Messenger (ﷺ) went out of the house and I sent Barīrah[18] after him to find out where he went." Barīrah returned to me and informed me that he (ﷺ) had gone to *Baqi'* graveyard, stood at its entrance with his hands raised, then he left. When I got up the next morning, I asked Allah's Messenger where he had gone the previous night and he replied,

---

[16] The second chapter of the Qur'an. The title, *al-Baqarah*, literally means 'the cow' and it refers to an incident mentioned in the chapter, verses 67-73.

[17] Muslim (English trans), vol. 1, p. 377, hadith no. 1707.

[18] 'Ā'ishah's servant-girl.

"*I was sent to the inhabitants of Baqi' to pray for them.*"[19]

6) Facing the Qiblah

During supplications for the dead, the grave should not be faced due to the general prohibition against prayer towards the graves. The supplicant should, instead, face Makkah when praying for the dead.

عَنْ أَبِي مَرْثَدٍ الْغَنَوِيِّ قَالَ سَمِعْتُ رَسُولَ اللَّهِ ﷺ يَقُولُ: ((لاَ تُصَلُّوا إِلَى الْقُبُورِ وَلاَ تَجْلِسُوا عَلَيْهَا)).

Abu Marthad al-Ghanawi quoted Allah's Messenger (ﷺ) as saying, "*Don't pray towards graves, nor sit on them.*"[20]

Since supplication (*du'ā*) is the essence of formal prayer, the ruling regarding the direction of prayer applies to both.

عَنِ النُّعْمَانِ بْنِ بَشِيرٍ عَنِ النَّبِيِّ صَلَّى اللَّهُ عَلَيْهِ وَسَلَّمَ قَالَ : ((الدُّعَاءُ هُوَ الْعِبَادَةُ ﴿ قَالَ رَبُّكُمُ ادْعُونِي أَسْتَجِبْ لَكُمْ ﴾))

An-Nu'mān ibn Bashīr related that the Prophet (ﷺ) said, "*Supplication is worship.*" Then he recited: ﴾Your Lord said: Call on Me and I will answer you.﴿[21] [22]

---

[19] *Musnad Aḥmad*, vol. 6, p. 92 and *Muwaṭṭa Imām Mālik*, p. 115, hadith no. 569 and authenticated in *Aḥkām al-Janā'iz*, Pp. 193-4. The 'raising of the hands' is not mentioned in *Muwaṭṭa Imām Mālik's* narration.

[20] Muslim (English trans), vol. 2, p. 460, hadith no. 2122 and *Sunan Abi Dāwūd*, vol. 2, p. 917, hadith no. 3223.

[21] *Soorah al-Ghāfir* (40):60.

[22] *Sunan Abi Dāwūd*, vol. 1, p. 387, hadith no. 1474 and by Bukhari in *al-Adab al-Mufrad*, hadith no. 714.

7) Walking Between the Graves

Shoes and sandals should be removed by those walking between the graves.

عَنْ بَشِيرٍ مَوْلَى رَسُولِ اللَّهِ ﷺ وَكَانَ اسْمُهُ فِي الْجَاهِلِيَّةِ زَحْمُ بْنُ مَعْبَدٍ فَهَاجَرَ إِلَى رَسُولِ اللَّهِ ﷺ فَقَالَ مَا اسْمُكَ قَالَ زَحْمٌ قَالَ بَلْ أَنْتَ بَشِيرٌ قَالَ بَيْنَمَا أَنَا أُمَاشِي رَسُولَ اللَّهِ ﷺ مَرَّ بِقُبُورِ الْمُشْرِكِينَ فَقَالَ: ((لَقَدْ سَبَقَ هَؤُلاَءِ خَيْرًا كَثِيرًا)) ثَلاَثًا ثُمَّ مَرَّ بِقُبُورِ الْمُسْلِمِينَ فَقَالَ: ((لَقَدْ أَدْرَكَ هَؤُلاَءِ خَيْرًا كَثِيرًا)) وَحَانَتْ مِنْ رَسُولِ اللَّهِ ﷺ نَظْرَةٌ فَإِذَا رَجُلٌ يَمْشِي فِي الْقُبُورِ عَلَيْهِ نَعْلاَنِ فَقَالَ: ((يَا صَاحِبَ السِّبْتِيَّتَيْنِ وَيْحَكَ أَلْقِ سِبْتِيَّتَيْكَ)) فَنَظَرَ الرَّجُلُ فَلَمَّا عَرَفَ رَسُولَ اللَّهِ ﷺ خَلَعَهُمَا فَرَمَى بِهِمَا.

Bashīr,[23] the freed slave of Allah's Messenger (ﷺ) said, "While I was walking with the Messenger of Allah (ﷺ), he passed by the graves of the pagans and said three times, "*They preceded a time of abundant good.*" Then he passed by the graves of the Muslims and said, "*They received abundant good.*" Allah's Messenger (ﷺ) then saw a man walking among the graves wearing sandals, so he called out, "*O you wearing sandals, beware. Remove your sandals.*" The man looked around and when he recognized Allah's Messenger (ﷺ), he took off his sandals and threw them away."[24]

---

[23] The narration explained that his pre-Islamic name was Zahm ibn Ma'bad. However, when the Prophet (ﷺ) was informed of his name, he renamed him 'Bashīr'.

[24] *Sunan Ibn Mājah*, vol. 2, Pp. 429-30, hadith no. 1568 and *Sunan Abi Dāwūd*, vol. 2, Pp. 917-8, hadith no. 3224 and authenticated by Shaykh al-Albāni in *Ṣaḥīḥ Sunan Abi Dāwūd*, vol. 2, p. 622, hadith no. 2767.

8) Annual Visits to Graves

Visiting graves, on the anniversary of a person's death, or at the time of special annual festivals of "saints" is forbidden.

عَنْ أَبِي هُرَيْرَةَ قَالَ قَالَ رَسُولُ اللَّهِ ﷺ : ((لاَ تَجْعَلُوا بُيُوتَكُمْ قُبُورًا وَلاَ تَجْعَلُوا قَبْرِي عِيدًا وَصَلُّوا عَلَيَّ فَإِنَّ صَلاَتَكُمْ تَبْلُغُنِي حَيْثُ كُنْتُمْ)).

Abu Hurayrah narrated that Allah's Messenger (ﷺ) said,

> *"Don't make your houses graveyards, nor make my grave a place of celebration*[25]*, and ask Allah's blessing for me, because it will reach me wherever you may be."*[26]

If the Prophet (ﷺ) prohibited the annual visiting of his grave, it goes without saying that the annual visiting of the graves of others is forbidden. Furthermore, the Prophet (ﷺ) limited Muslim annual festivals to two and cancelled all others.

عَنْ أَنَسٍ قَالَ قَدِمَ رَسُولُ اللَّهِ ﷺ الْمَدِينَةَ وَلَهُمْ يَوْمَانِ يَلْعَبُونَ فِيهِمَا فَقَالَ : ((مَا هَذَانِ الْيَوْمَانِ)) قَالُوا : كُنَّا نَلْعَبُ فِيهِمَا فِي الْجَاهِلِيَّةِ فَقَالَ رَسُولُ اللَّهِ ﷺ : ((إِنَّ اللَّهَ قَدْ أَبْدَلَكُمْ بِهِمَا خَيْرًا مِنْهُمَا يَوْمَ الأَضْحَى وَيَوْمَ الْفِطْرِ)).

Anas related that when Allah's Messenger (ﷺ) came to Madīnah, the people had two days (annually) in which they used to enjoy themselves with games. He asked, "*What are these two days?*" They said, "*We used to play games on them during the pre-Islamic period.*" Allah's Messenger (ﷺ) said,

---

[25] The term used in the hadith is *'eed*, i.e., an annual celebration.

[26] *Sunan Abi Dāwūd*, vol. 2, Pp. 542-3, hadith no. 2037 and authenticated by Shaykh al-Albāni in *Ṣaḥīḥ Sunan Abi Dāwūd*, vol. 1, p. 383, hadith no. 1796.

> *"Allah has substituted them with something better than them: 'Eed al-Aḍḥā (Festival of Sacrifice) and 'Eed al-Fiṭr (Festival of Fast Breaking)."*[27]

9) Travelling to Visit Graves

Setting out on journeys to visit graves was specifically forbidden by the Prophet (ﷺ). This practice forms the basis of idolatrous pilgrimages in other religions.

عَنْ أَبِي هُرَيْرَةَ رَضِي اللَّهُ عَنْهُ عَنِ النَّبِيِّ ﷺ قَالَ: ((لاَ تُشَدُّ الرِّحَالُ إِلاَّ إِلَى ثَلاَثَةِ مَسَاجِدَ الْمَسْجِدِ الْحَرَامِ وَمَسْجِدِ الرَّسُولِ ﷺ وَمَسْجِدِ الأَقْصَى)).

Abu Hurayrah quoted the Prophet (ﷺ) as saying,

> *"Do not set out on (religious) journeys except to three masjids: al-Masjid al-Ḥarām (Makkah), Masjid ar-Rasūl (Madīnah) and Masjid al-Aqṣā (Jerusalem)."*[28]

While returning from a trip, Abu Baṣrah al-Ghifāri met Abu Hurayrah and the latter asked him where he was coming from. Abu Baṣrah replied that he was coming back from *aṭ-Ṭūr*[29] where he had made prayer. Abu Hurayrah said, "If only I had caught you before you had set out, for I heard Allah's Messenger (ﷺ) say: *Don't travel (for religious purposes) to other than three*

---

[27] *Sunan Abi Dāwūd*, vol. 1, p. 293, hadith no. 1130 and authenticated by Shaykh al-Albāni in *Ṣaḥīḥ Sunan Abi Dāwūd*, vol. 1, p. 210, hadith no. 1003.

[28] Bukhari (Arabic-English), vol. 1, p. 157, hadith no. 281, Muslim (English trans), vol. 2, p. 699, hadith no. 3218, and *Sunan Abi Dāwūd*, vol. 2, p. 540, hadith no. 2028.

[29] *Aṭ-Ṭūr* is the mountain mentioned in the Qur'an, 2:60, generally understood to be Mount *Sinai* (*Dictionary of Islam*, p. 647 and *Arabic-English Lexicon*, vol. 2, p. 1890).

masjids..."[30] Abu Qaz'ah also related that he had wanted to go to *aṭ-Ṭūr*, but when he asked Ibn 'Umar about it, he quoted the Prophet's prohibition of (religious) travel to other than the three masjids.[31]

10) Planting Twigs on Graves

It is not permissible to plant any flowers or twigs on the grave. The placing of wreaths and flowers is a non-Muslim ritual. The Companions of the Prophet (ﷺ) and the early generation of Muslim scholars did not practice this ritual. It is, however, authentically narrated that the Prophet (ﷺ) did, on one single occasion, stick a palm leaf in a grave.

عَنِ ابْنِ عَبَّاسٍ رَضِيَ اللَّهُ عَنْهُمَا عَنِ النَّبِيِّ ﷺ أَنَّهُ مَرَّ بِقَبْرَيْنِ يُعَذَّبَانِ فَقَالَ : ((إِنَّهُمَا لَيُعَذَّبَانِ وَمَا يُعَذَّبَانِ فِي كَبِيرٍ أَمَّا أَحَدُهُمَا فَكَانَ لاَ يَسْتَتِرُ مِنَ الْبَوْلِ وَأَمَّا الآخَرُ فَكَانَ يَمْشِي بِالنَّمِيمَةِ)) ثُمَّ أَخَذَ جَرِيدَةً رَطْبَةً فَشَقَّهَا بِنِصْفَيْنِ ثُمَّ غَرَزَ فِي كُلِّ قَبْرٍ وَاحِدَةً فَقَالُوا يَا رَسُولَ اللَّهِ، لِمَ صَنَعْتَ هَذَا فَقَالَ : ((لَعَلَّهُ أَنْ يُخَفَّفَ عَنْهُمَا مَا لَمْ يَيْبَسَا)).

Ibn 'Abbās reported that the Prophet (Blessings and Peace be upon him) once passed by the graves of two people who were being punished in their graves and said, "*They are not being punished for a major sin. One didn't use to protect himself from the splatter of urine and the other used to spread rumours.*" He then took a green leaf of a date-palm tree, split it into two pieces, and planted one on each grave. The people asked, "O Messenger of Allah! Why have you done this?" He replied,

---

[30] *Musnad Aḥmad* (6/7) and authenticated in *Aḥkām al-Janā'iz*, p. 226.

[31] Collected by al-Azraqi in *Akhbār Makkah*, p. 304 and authenticated in *Aḥkām al-Janā'iz*, p. 226.

> *"Perhaps it will reduce their punishment as long as it remains green."*[32]

In Jābir's narration the Prophet (ﷺ) said,

((إِنِّي مَرَرْتُ بِقَبْرَيْنِ يُعَذَّبَانِ، فَأَحْبَبْتُ بِشَفَاعَتِي أَنْ يُرَفَّهَ عَنْهُمَا مَا دَامَ الْغُصْنَانِ رَطْبَيْنِ))

> *"I passed by two graves whose occupants were being tormented. I wished to make intercession for them (so I placed two twigs on their graves) so that they may be relieved as long as these two twigs remain fresh."*[33]

Planting leaves in a grave was an act unique to the Prophet (ﷺ), consequently, none of his early followers repeated it. The tenth century CE hadith scholar, al-Khaṭṭābi,[34] said the following regarding this hadith, "It represents the (principle that the) actions of the Prophet (ﷺ) are blessed and that his supplication to lessen their punishment is special to Allah. He also chose the period of freshness of the leaf to be (the length of) the period of his request for a reduction (in their punishment). This does not mean that a fresh leaf has any superiority over a dry leaf. It is now the custom among the masses in many countries to plant palm leaves in the graves of their dead. However, what they are doing cannot be

---

[32] Bukhari (Arabic-English), vol. 2, Pp. 249-50, hadith no. 443 and Muslim (English trans), vol. 1, Pp. 171-2, hadith no. 575.

[33] Muslim (English trans), vol. 4, Pp. 1545-9, hadith no. 7149. This text is on page 1548.

[34] Abu Sulaymān Ḥamad ibn Muhammad al-Khaṭṭābi (925-1010 CE) was born in the town of Bost, in southern Afghanistan close to the modern town of Lashkar Gah. He travelled to Naishapur, Baghdad, Makkah and Baṣrah. In Naishapur he wrote *Gharīb al-Hadith, Ma'ālim as-Sunan* (Commentary on *Sunan Abi Dāwūd*), and a commentary on *Ṣaḥīḥ al-Bukhari* (*Siyar A'lām an-Nubalā*, vol. 17, Pp. 23-28).

based on the Prophet's act." Aḥmad Shākir in his commentary on the hadith compilation, *Sunan at-Tirmidhi,* said, "Al-Khaṭṭābi spoke the truth. And, since that time, the (Muslim) masses have become even more devoted to this practice which has no valid basis in Islam. The (ignorant Muslim masses) imitate the Christians so much, especially in Egypt, that they now put flowers on the graves and exchange them as presents among themselves. Some people put them on the graves of their relatives and friends as greetings to them and as a courtesy to their living relatives similar to the international etiquette of courtesy to the dead. Thus, whenever Muslim personalities visit a European country, they go to the graves of its former leaders or the grave of the 'unknown soldier' and lay fresh and artificial wreaths of flowers on them."[35]

This practice is an innovation in the religion (*bid'ah*) which should be avoided. All such innovations are cursed. Ibn 'Umar is reported to have said, in this regard,

كُلُّ بِدْعَةٍ ضَلاَلَةٌ، وَإِنْ رآهَا النَّاسُ حَسَنَةً.

"Every innovation is misguidance, even if people consider them to be good."[36]

---

[35] *Sunan at-Tirmidhi*, vol. 1, p. 103 quoted in *Aḥkām al-Janā'iz*, p. 200.

[36] Collected by Ibn Baṭṭah in *Al-Ibānah 'an Uṣūl ad-Diyānah*, vol. 2, p. 112, hadith no. 2 and authenticated in *Aḥkām al-Janā'iz*, Pp. 200-1.

based on the [illegible] and [illegible] the Hadith [illegible] spoke [illegible] become [illegible] for this [illegible] basis [illegible] ignorant Muslims [illegible] Christians [illegible], especially in Egypt, [illegible] on the graves and exchange them as presents [illegible]. Some people put flowers on the graves of [illegible] as greetings [illegible] courtesy [illegible] similar to the [illegible] etiquette of [illegible] whenever Muslim personalities visit a [illegible] to the graves of its former leaders or the tomb of the unknown soldier, and this is an [illegible] them.

This practice is an innovation in the [illegible] which should be avoided. All such innovation [illegible] reported to have said in this regard:

[illegible]

"Every innovation is misguidance, even if people consider them to be good."

[illegible]

Collected by Ibn Battah in *Al-Ibanah*, [illegible] hadith no. 2 [illegible] *Ahkam al-Jana'iz* [illegible]

APPENDIX: INNOVATIONS

The following is a list of common funeral-related innovations practiced by Muslims in different parts of the world:

1. Turning the dying person's body to face the Qiblah.
2. The removal of menstruating women from a dead or dying person's presence.
3. Leaving dying men among the women and only coming to collect their bodies after they have died.
4. Recital of the Qur'an for money at the time of the person's death.
5. Placing lit candles near the dead body until the morning.
6. Putting cotton in the throat, nostrils, and anus of the dead person.
7. Clipping the fingernails of the dead body and shaving its pubic hair.
8. Recital of *Sūrah al-Fātiḥah*, *al-Baqarah* and the last two verses of *Sūrah al-Baqarah* based on a fabricated narration falsely attributed to Ibn 'Umar.[1]

---

[1] 'Abdullah ibn 'Umar is reported to have said that he heard the Prophet (ﷺ) say, "*When one of you dies, do not keep his body for long, but take him quickly to his grave, and have the opening verses of sūrah al-Baqarah recited at his head and the concluding verses of the same sūrah recited at his feet.*" (Collected by al-Bayhaqi in *Shu'ab al-Eemān*. See *Mishkāt al-Maṣābīḥ*, vol. 1, p. 358).

9. "Whoever recites the *Sūrah al-Ikhlās* 1000 times will be safeguarded from Hell," is a fabricated tradition.

10. Instructing (*talqīn*) those who have already died to recite the declaration of faith *lā ilāha il-lal-lāh.*[2]

11. Writing *du'ās* on the shroud.

12. Making absent funeral prayers (*ṣalātul-ghā'ib*) for people for whom funeral prayers were made in the location in which they died.

13. Transferring the body of the deceased over long distances in order to bury the person near the graves of the pious or in their home countries.

14. Reciting Qur'an aloud, poems or words of remembrance while carrying the bier.

15. Excessive talking in loud voices during the time of burial.

16. Sprinkling rose water when placing the body in the grave and everybody covering the grave with sand while reciting specific prayers.

17. Recitation of the *Shahādah* 3 times after closing the grave and sprinkling water on it.

18. Placing flowers, twigs etc. on the graves based on Prophet Muhammad's action.[3] What the Prophet (ﷺ) did was special

---

[2] This practice is of no use to the dead. The Prophet (ﷺ) recommended that those who are dying should be encouraged to recite the declaration of faith.

[3] Ibn 'Abbās reported that the Prophet (ﷺ) once passed by the graves of two people who were being punished in their graves and said, "*They are not being punished for major sins; one regularly didn't protect himself from the splatter of his urine and the other used to spread rumours.*" He then took a green leaf of a date-palm tree, split it into two pieces, and planted one on each grave.=

for him and he did not do it for every grave.

19. Building structures over graves or placing grave stones to indicate the name and family of the dead.

20. Commemorating the 1st, 3rd, 7th, 20th, or 40th day following someone's death.

21. Gathering at the home of the dead person and obliging the family of the deceased to provide food for the guests.

22. Reciting of the *Adhān at the graveyard. How this practice came into being is unknown especially when there is no Adhān or Iqāmah* for the funeral prayer.

23. Recital of *Sūrah Yasīn* at the graveyard.

24. Putting flag poles with white flags outside the home of one who has died to indicate that death has occurred in the family. This is a practice of Hindu origin found amongst Muslims in Southern Philippines.

25. Avoiding the celebration of *'Eed* because of death in the family. Refusing to visit people on *'Eed* for the same reason.

26. Visiting the graves of one's parents every *Jumu'ah*.

27. Visiting the graves in the middle of the month of Sha'bān.

28. Visiting the graves specifically every *'Eed*, or in the months of Rajab, Sha'bān or Ramaḍān.

29. Dedicating the reward for certain acts of worship like *ṣalāh,* and Qur'anic recitation to the dead or to the Prophet (ﷺ).

=The people asked, "O Messenger of Allah! Why have you done this?" He replied, "*Perhaps it will reduce their punishment as long as it remains green.*" [Bukhari (Arabic-English), vol. 2, Pp. 249-50, hadith no. 443].

30. Circumambulating the Prophet's (ﷺ) grave or any other grave.

31. Touching or wiping the tombs of the righteous in the belief that blessings will be gained from this act.

BIBLIOGRAPHY

Abbasi, S.M. Madni, *Riyadh-uṣ-Ṣaleḥīn,* Riyadh: International Islamic Publishing House, n.d.

Albānī, Muhammad Nāṣirud-Dīn al-, *Aḥkām al-Janā'iz,* Beirut: al-Maktab al-Islami, 8th ed.,1986.

..............................., *Ṣaḥīḥ Sunan Abi Dāwūd*, Beirut: al-Maktab al-Islami, 1st. ed., 1989.

..............................., *Ṣaḥīḥ Sunan an-Nasā'i,* Beirut: al-Maktab al-Islami, 1st. ed., 1988.

..............................., *Ṣaḥīḥ Sunan at-Tirmidhi,* Beirut: al-Maktab al-Islami, 1st. ed., 1988.

..............................., *Ṣaḥīḥ Sunan Ibn Mājah,* Beirut: al-Maktab al-Islami, 3rd. ed., 1988.

'Alā'i, Abu Sa'īd ibn Khalīl al-. *Jāmi' at-Taḥṣīl fi Aḥkām al-Marāsīl*. Beirut: Maktabah an-Nahḍah al-'Arabīyah, 1987.

'Awn al-Ma'būd: *Sharḥ Sunan abi Dāwūd*, Beirut: Dār Ehiya al-Tourath al-Arabi, 2001.

Adhīmābādi, Muhammad Ashraf al-, *'Awn al-Ma'būd: Sharḥ Sunan Abi Dāwūd,* Beirut: Dār al-Kutub al-'Ilmīyah, 1990.

Anṣari, Muhammad Tufail, *Sunan Ibn-i-Mājah (Arabic-English)*, Lahore: Kazi Publications, 1st. ed., 1993.

Baghawi, al-Ḥusayn ibn Mas'ūd al-, *Sharḥ as-Sunnah,* Beirut: al-Maktab al-Islami, 2nd. ed., 1983.

Bashīr, Zakaria, *Sunshine at Madīnah,* United Kingdom: The Islamic Foundation, 1990.

Glasse, Cyril, *The Concise Encyclopaedia of Islam,* London: Stacey International, 1989.

Guillaume, A., *The Life of Muhammad,* Karachi: Oxford University Press, 1st. ed., 1955.

Ḥasan, Aḥmad, *Sunan Abu Dāwūd,* (English Trans.), Lahore: Sh. Muhammad Ashraf Publishers, 1st ed., 1987.

Hughes, Thomas Patrick, *Dictionary of Islam,* Lahore: Premier Book House, reprinted 1989.

Ibn al-Athīr, *an-Nihāyah fi Gharīb al-Hadith wal-Athar,* Beirut: al-Maktabah al-'Ilmīyah, 1963.

Ibn Ḥajar, Aḥmad ibn 'Ali, *Fatḥ al-Bāri,* Cairo: Dār Abi Ḥayyān, 1st ed., 1996.

Ibn Ḥazm, 'Ali ibn Aḥmad, *al-Muhallā,* Beirut: Dār al-Āfāq al-Jadīdah, n.d.

Ibn Qudāmah, 'Abdullah ibn Aḥmad, *al-Mughni,* Cairo: Hajar Press, 1989.

Khan, Muhammad Muḥsin, *Ṣaḥīḥ al-Bukhari,* (Arabic-English), Lahore: Kazi Publications, 6th ed., 1986.

Lane, E.W., *Arabic-English Lexicon,* Cambridge, England: Islamic Texts Society, 1984.

Nawawi, Yaḥyā ibn Sharaf an-, *Al-Majmū',*. Jeddah: *Maktabah al-Irshād*, n.d.

................................., *Ṣaḥīḥ Kitāb al-Adhkār,* (edited by Salīm al-Hilāli), Madīnah: *Maktab al-Ghurabā al-Atharīyah*, 1413 AH.

Raḥimuddin, Muhammad, *Muwaṭṭa Imām Mālik,* (English Trans.), Lahore: Sh. Muhammad Ashraf Publishers, 1980.

Robson, James, *Mishkāt al-Maṣābīḥ,* (English Trans.), Lahore: Sh. Muhammad Ashraf, 1981.

Ṣiddiqi, 'Abdul Ḥamid, *Ṣaḥīḥ Muslim,* (English Trans.), Lahore: Sh. Muhammad Ashraf Publishers, 1987.

Shawkāni, Muhammad ibn 'Ali, ash-, *Nayl al-Awtār,* Cairo, Egypt: Dār al-Hadith, 1993.

Dhahabi, Muhammad ibn Aḥmad adh-, *Siyar A'lām an-Nubalā*, Beirut: Mu'assasah ar-Risālah, 8th ed., 1992.

Zirikli, Khayrud-dīn, az-, *Al-A'lām,* Beirut: 1969.

CD - Roms:

Al-Hadith ash-Sharīf. Beirut: Ariss Computer, n.d.

[illegible] (English Trans.). Lahore: Sh. Muhammad Ashraf Publishers, 1980.

Robson, James. [illegible] (English Trans.). Lahore: Sh. Muhammad Ashraf, 1981.

Siddiqi, Abdul Hamid. Sahih Muslim (English Trans.). Lahore: Sh. Muhammad Ashraf Publishers, 198[illegible].

Shawkani, Muhammad Ibn 'Ali, ash-. [illegible]. Beyrut: Dar al-[illegible], 1973.

[illegible] Muhammad Ibn Ahmad al-. [illegible]. [illegible] 5th ed., 1992.

Zarkali, Khayr ad-Din az-. Al-A'lam. Beirut, 198[illegible].

CD - Roms

Al-Hadith ash-Sharif. Beirut: Arees Computer, n.d.

GLOSSARY

Aḥkām al-Janā'iz	أحكام الجنائز	:	Rulings about funeral
Al-Baqi'	البقيع	:	The name given to the graveryard of the city of Madīnah
Al-Ḥidād	الحِداد	:	Mourning
'Asab	عسب	:	Yemeni cloth made from partially dyed yarn
Bid'ah	بدعه	:	Innovation in religion
Dhikr	ذِكر	:	Lit. Remembrance, remembering Allah's names, attributes, reciting the Qur'an
Du'ā	دعاء	:	Supplication
Farḍ	فرض	:	Compulsory
Farḍ Kifāyah	فرض الكفاية	:	Collective obligation
Fiqh	فقه	:	Islamic Jurisprudence
Fitnah	فتنه	:	Trial
Ghārimūn	غارمون	:	Debtors
Ghusl	غُسل	:	Islamic bath
Hadith Qudsi	حديث قدسى	:	Non-Qur'anic revealed words of Allah through the last Prophet
Ḥarām	حرام	:	Not permissible, in Islamic law (*shari'ah*)

Hijrah	هجرة	:	The Prophet and his Makkan Companions' migration from Makkah to the city of Madīnah
Iḥrām	احرام	:	*Iḥrām* represents the consecrated state of one who has made the intention for either the greater or lesser pilgrimage — Ḥajj or 'Umrah and has put on the specified garments, consisting of a cloak and waist-wrapper. Men are not allowed to cover their heads when in this consecrated state.
Jamā'ah	جماعة	:	Congregation, congregational prayer
Kufr	كفر	:	Disbelief
Laḥd	لحد	:	Niche
Najis	نجس	:	Ritually impure according to Islam
Nifāq	نفاق	:	Hypocricy, subtle disbelief
Qiblah	قبله	:	Ka'bah in Makkah, Muslims are to face it while praying
Ramy	رمى	:	Stoning the *Jamarāt* during Ḥajj
Ṣadaqah	صدقه	:	Charity, also zakah
Ṣalāḥ	صلاة / صلوة	:	Prayer obligatory/optional
Ṣalatul-Janāzah	صلاة الجنازة	:	The funeral prayer
Shahādah	شهاده	:	Witness, saying *la ilāha il-lal-lāh*
Shahīd	شهيد	:	Martyr in the way of Allah

Sūrah al-Baqarah	سورة البقره	:	The second chapter of the Qur'an. The title, *al-Baqarah*, literally means 'the cow' and it refers to an incident mentioned in the chapter, verses 67-73
Sūrah Yasīn	سورة يسٓ	:	36th chapter of the Qur'an
Tābi'īn	تابعون	:	Sing. *Tābi'i*: The Followers — the students and followers of the Companions of the Prophet Muhammad (ﷺ)
Takbīr	تكبير	:	Saying *Allahu Akbar* — Allah is All-Great
Talbīnah	تلبينه	:	Porridge made from flour, bran and honey
Talbiyah	تلبيه	:	*Talbiyah* is the supplication repeated aloud by pilgrims at the beginning of 'Umrah or Ḥajj and during their journey to Makkah.
Taslīm	تسليم	:	The act of completing the formal prayer by giving greetings of *salām* (peace); saying *Assalāmu Alaykum wa Raḥmatullah*
Tawḥīd	توحيد	:	The belief in the Oneness of Divinity of Allah
Uḥud	أحد	:	*Uḥud* is a volcanic hill with a plain stretching before it on the western outskirts of Madīnah. The Quraysh defeated the Muslims there in the third year of the *Hijrah* (625 CE).

Ummah	أمه	:	Nation
Waṣiyyah	وصية	:	Will
Zakah	زكوة / زكاة	:	An annual obligatory prescribed charity (or poor due) by a Muslim in possession of riches, merchandise, agricultural produce, livestock, trading goods etc. over a prescribed limit — a certain minimum called *niṣāb*. A pillar of Islam. Rate of payment varies according to the kind of possession. Details to be found in *Fiqh* books. Way of distribution to be found in the Qur'an 9:60.

TRANSLITERATION CHART

أ	a
آ - ى	ā
ب	b
ت	t
ة	h or t (when followed by another Arabic word)
ث	th
ج	j
ح	ḥ
خ	kh
د	d
ذ	dh
ر	r
ز	z
س	s
ش	sh
ص	ṣ
ض	ḍ
ط	ṭ

ظ	<u>dh</u>
ع	‘
غ	gh
ف	f
ق	q
ك	k
ل	l
م	m
ن	n
هـ – ه – ـه	h
و	w
و (as vowel)	ū or oo
ي	y
ي (as vowel)	ī or ee
ء	’ (Omitted in initial position)

ـَ	Fatḥah	a
ـِ	Kasra	i
ـُ	Ḍammah	u
ـّ	Shaddah	Double letter
ـْ	Sukūn	Absence of vowel

SYMBOLS' DIRECTORY

(سُبْحَانَهُ وَتَعَالَىٰ) : *Subḥānahu wa Ta'āla* — "The Exalted."

(صَلَّى اللهُ عَلَيْهِ وَسَلَّمَ) : *Ṣalla-Allahu 'Alayhi wa Sallam* —
"Blessings and Peace be upon him."

(عَلَيْهِ السَّلَامُ) : *'Alayhis-Salām* — "May Peace be upon him."

(رَضِيَ اللهُ عَنْهُ) : *Raḍi-Allahu 'Anhu* — "May Allah be pleased with him."